"*To All the World* is an important book that explores how preaching is essential to the New Evangelization. The essays are practical, inviting the reader to consider how every aspect of one's life should be a preaching of Jesus Christ to the world. The breadth of cultural and ministerial backgrounds is unique to this volume. The reader will be inspired to think anew about the ministry of preaching through the edited essays."

—Timothy P. O'Malley
Director, Notre Dame Center for Liturgy

"It is no accident that people are drawn to Pope Francis' simple, appealing preaching of the good news of Jesus Christ. *To All the World* captures that same spirit. Chronicling the University of Notre Dame Conference, in which I happily participated, Fr. Connors presents the fine array of speakers who return to the same theme: Preach Jesus Christ to the world—with continuity and creativity—and let the grace of Christ attract the world to sit up, listen attentively, and follow in His steps."

—Most Reverend Joseph E. Kurtz, DD
Archbishop of Louisville
President, United States Conference of Catholic Bishops

"Preaching is such a personal endeavor that it takes a wide range of writers to cover its multiple aspects. Connors has masterfully gathered a roomful of opinions and experiences to share insights about the mystery and power of preaching the gospel."

—Rev. Paul Turner
Pastor, St. Anthony Catholic Church in Kansas City Missouri
Contributor, *To All the World*

D0886259

To All the World

Preaching and the New Evangelization

edited by Michael E. Connors, CSC

LITURGICAL PRESS
Collegeville, Minnesota

www.litpress.org

1   2   3   4   5   6   7   8   9

Library of Congress Cataloging-in-Publication Data

Names: Connors, Michael E., editor.
Title: To all the world : preaching and the new evangelization / edited by
    Michael E. Connors.
Description: Collegeville, Minnesota : Liturgical Press, 2016.
Identifiers: LCCN 2015040838 | ISBN 9780814647080 | ISBN 9780814647332 (ebook)
Subjects: LCSH: Catholic preaching. | Evangelistic work—Catholic Church.
Classification: LCC BX1795.P72 T6 2016 | DDC 251—dc23
LC record available at http://lccn.loc.gov/2015040838

Contents

Preface

The church, said Pope Paul VI, "exists in order to evangelize, that is to say, in order to preach and teach, to be the channel of the gift of grace, to reconcile sinners with God, and to perpetuate Christ's sacrifice in the Mass, which is the memorial of His death and glorious resurrection."[1] "The task of evangelizing all people constitutes the essential mission of the Church."[2] *Evangelii Nuntiandi* single-handedly breathed new life into Catholic missiology and homiletics. The text repays careful attention even today, forty years later.

More than thirty years ago now, Pope John Paul II famously summoned the church to "a New Evangelization, new in its ardor, methods and expression."[3] John Paul devoted much of his long papacy to infusing this project with clarity and energy. He emphasized that the message, the Gospel of Jesus Christ, is not new, but the same life-giving announcement that has moved hearts, lit minds, and fired wills for twenty centuries. But devotion flags and needs to be renewed. Technologies and social patterns change, opening up new vehicles for the proclamation of God's goodness. New cultural contexts are reached, and old ones change, demanding fresh ways of presenting the invitation to discipleship.

Pope Benedict XVI continued to speak about the urgency of a New Evangelization, especially in contexts formerly regarded as Christian, where the corrosive influences of contemporary culture are strong. "At the dawn of the third millennium," he noted, "not only are there still many peoples who have not come to know the Good News, but also a great many Christians who need to have the word of God once more persuasively proclaimed to them, so that they can concretely experience the power of the Gospel. Many of our brothers and sisters are 'baptized, but insufficiently evangelized.'" The New Evangelization must be brought to bear "especially in those nations where the Gospel has been forgotten or meets with indifference as a result of widespread secularism."[4]

The first pope from the "global South," Pope Francis has infused a special kind of vigor into the New Evangelization through his own preaching, both in the Vatican and in his far-flung travels. He has reminded us that the Gospel is a message of joy, and the task of proclamation a privilege. "Instead of seeming to impose new obligations," Francis wrote, "[Christians] should appear as people who wish to share their joy, who point to a horizon of beauty and who invite others to a delicious banquet."[5] Francis has also reemphasized a theme of the Second Vatican Council, namely, that all Christians share in the project of evangelization: "In virtue of their baptism, all the members of the People of God have become missionary disciples (cf. Mt 28:19). All the baptized, whatever their position in the Church or their level of instruction in the faith, are agents of evangelization. . . . The new evangelization calls for personal involvement on the part of each of the baptized. Every Christian is challenged, here and now, to be actively engaged in evangelization" (*Evangelii Gaudium* 120).[6]

The present volume grew out of a conference of the same name at the University of Notre Dame in June 2014. Speakers, preachers, bishops, evangelizers, lay and ordained, men and women—there was a palpable sense of devotion to the church's evangelical mission as we gathered. One after another the speakers thoughtfully put flesh on the bone of "new ardor, new methods, and new expressions." Fidelity to tradition and creative willingness to risk new strategies, love for the Word and love for God's people, zeal for the universality of the message and deep respect for the plurality of cultures and religious faiths—these were but some of the tensions into which we stepped, gaining confidence that each may yet yield the precious Gospel fruit of hope for our battered, divided world.

"The Church, sure of her Lord's fidelity, never tires of proclaiming the good news of the Gospel and invites all Christians to discover anew the attraction of following Christ."[7]

Michael E. Connors, CSC
John S. Marten Program in Homiletics and
    Liturgics, University of Notre Dame
Easter season, 2015

Endnotes

1. Paul VI, *Evangelii Nuntiandi* (Washington, DC: USCCB, 1975) 14.

2. Ibid. Paul VI is quoting the 1974 Synod of Bishops; see "Declaration of the Synod Fathers," 4, *L'Osservatore Romano* (27 October 1974): 6.

3. Address to CELAM (Opening Address of the Nineteenth General Assembly of CELAM, 9 March 1983, Port-au-Prince, Haiti), *L'Osservatore Romano*, English Edition 16/780 (18 April 1983): 9.

4. Benedict XVI, *Verbum Domini* (The Word of the Lord) (Vatican City: Libreria Editrice Vaticana, 2010) 96, 122. The interior quote is from the previous year's synod of bishops on the Word of God, *Propositio* 38.

5. Pope Francis, *Evangelii Gaudium* (The Joy of the Gospel) (Vatican City: Libreria Editrice Vaticana, 2013) 15, http://w2.vatican.va/content/francesco/en/apost _exhortations/documents/papa-francesco_esortazione-ap_20131124_evangelii -gaudium.html.

6. See also Gregory Heille, OP, *The Preaching of Pope Francis: Missionary Discipleship and the Ministry of the Word* (Collegeville, MN: Liturgical Press, 2015).

7. Benedict XVI, *Verbum Domini* 96.

Chapter 1

Preaching: Conversation in Friendship

Timothy Radcliffe, OP

Anthony Trollope, the nineteenth-century English novelist, said, "There is, perhaps, no greater hardship at present inflicted on mankind in civilized and free countries, than the necessity of listening to sermons."[1] Even committed Christians often find listening to preachers an exquisite torture. An Irish priest, who is a wonderful preacher, told me that after he has been preaching for just three minutes, invariably a large and threatening parishioner will rise to his feet and point dramatically at his watch. In whatever way we share our faith, in the pulpit or in the classroom or on the web, we shall have to break through a barrier of indifference, especially in Europe. Those banners that one sees outside churches—"Repent and believe in the gospel" or "God is love"—fail to touch the imagination of anyone who does not already believe. Bare words are not enough. This is the challenge for evangelization.

The most beautiful story of how this may happen is, of course, the journey to Emmaus of disciples utterly oblivious to the presence of Jesus (Luke 24:13-35). Two things heal their blindness. First of all there is the joy: "Were not our hearts burning [within us] while he spoke to us on the way and opened the scriptures to us?" But it was his gesture of breaking bread that finally opened their eyes.

Let's begin with the joy. They experience that joy even before they know who he is and why they are happy. They feel it even while they are still

1

walking in the wrong direction. Jesus does not block their path or refuse to go with them. He does not jump up and down and say, "You are going the wrong way!" He shares their mistaken journey. But it is the joy that prepares them to hear the Gospel and return to the community in Jerusalem. It is the joy of John the Baptist who leaped in the womb of Elizabeth before he could even see the face of Jesus. The joy is the pre-evangelization. It is not a hearty, backslapping jollity. What is it, then?

In the *De Catechizandis Rudibus*, St. Augustine said that the teacher should communicate with *hilaritas*. This is usually translated as "cheerfulness," which suggests that we should liven things up with a few jokes. I have nothing against that and do it myself. But *hilaritas* here means something more like exuberance, an ecstatic joy. When teaching takes off, we are exhilarated, carried out of ourselves. This hilarity is an experience of grace. It liberates us from self-preoccupation; it is a first encounter with the Lord. It is a foretaste of our ultimate destiny, the joy of God. Everything begins in the inarticulate joy of those who have not yet found words, and ends with the joy of those who have left the words behind them.

Cornelius Ernst, OP, talked of grace as "the genetic moment": "Every genetic moment is a mystery. It is dawn, discovery, spring, new birth, coming to the light, awakening, transcendence, liberation, ecstasy, bridal consent, gift, forgiveness, reconciliation, revolution, faith, hope, love. It could be said that Christianity is the consecration of the genetic moment, the living center from which it reviews the indefinitely various and shifting perspectives of human experience in history. That, at least, is or ought to be its claim: that it is the power to transform and renew all things: 'Behold, I make all things new' (Rev. 21, 5)."[2] *Hilaritas* is an experience of this fertile, ever-new grace.

The disciples experienced this *hilaritas* in conversation with Jesus. Conversation is the typical mode of Christian evangelization. Saint Augustine, the greatest preacher of the West, conversed with his congregation, argued with them, joked with them, answered objections, posed questions. His sermons take off in this interchange, the preacher and the people igniting each other. We rub each other up the right way. A famous Dominican of my province, Vincent McNabb, argued vigorously with a woman when he was preaching at Speakers' Corner in London. She said, "Oh Father, if I was married to you, I would poison you." To which he replied, "Madame, if I was married to you, I would take it."

We may preach in all imaginable ways: sermons, articles, books, blogs, or broadcasts. But evangelization is not the communication of information but an event, a happening of grace, a sharing in the pregnancy of Mary and the fertility of Easter. But nothing will happen, unless it is rooted in the conversation, the to-and-fro of debate, the mutual exchange in which we both speak and listen and set each other alight. Why is this conversation the context of all effective evangelization?

First of all, because no communication is Christian that does not respect the dignity of the people whom we address. A rhetoric that whips people up but does not treat them as free subjects, equal interlocutors, could not be a preaching of the Gospel. James Alison writes about what he calls Nuremburg worship, which suppresses individuality and transforms the community into a mob: "You bring people together and you unite them in worship. You provide regular rhythmic music and marching. You enable them to see lots of people in uniform, people who have already lost a certain individuality and become symbols. You give them songs to sing. . . . All this serves to take people out of themselves; the normally restrained become passionate, unfriendly neighbors find themselves looking at each other anew in the light of the growing 'Bruderschaft.'"[3] They get swallowed up in the mob. Every mob can become a lynch mob. On Palm Sunday, they sang hosannas. On Good Friday, they cried, "Crucify him."

Secondly, revelation *is* the conversation of God with his people. In *Verbum Domini*, Pope Benedict wrote, "The novelty of biblical revelation consists in the fact that God becomes known through the dialogue which he desires to have with us" (6). The life of God is the eternal dialogue of the Father and the Son in the Spirit. Revelation is God's invitation to us to be at home in that eternal, equal loving conversation. Benedict again: "The Word, who from the beginning is with God and is God, reveals God himself in the dialogue of love between the divine persons, and invites us to share in that love" (ibid.). Revelation is not about receiving messages from a divine outer space. It is being taken up into the eternal conversation that is the life of God. Herbert McCabe compared this to the elation of conversation in a Dublin pub! And so we can only share our faith in conversation. The medium is the message.

Good conversation demands two things that are necessarily in tension: you have something to say and something to learn. If you have nothing to say, then the conversation will be vacuous. If you have nothing to learn, then it will swiftly become a monologue or a shouting match. Evangelization happens when there is the right dynamic between these two. Jesus listens to the conversation of the disciples on the way to Emmaus, and then teaches them.

We Christians have a teaching to give. Our faith is doctrinal. At the end of Matthew's gospel, Jesus sends out the disciples to teach all that they have learned from him. But our society resists our teaching since it is a doctrine of the Enlightenment that doctrine is infantile, suppressing freedom of thought. There is a dogmatic rejection of doctrine. But, as G. K. Chesterton once remarked, "There are only two kinds of people, those who accept dogmas and know it, and those who accept dogmas and don't. . . . Trees have no dogmas. Turnips are singularly broadminded."[4]

This prejudice against Christian doctrine has so saturated our culture that it is shared by most Catholics. It is usually accepted as a condition of membership of the church, but few people get excited by doctrine. Spirituality is more popular. It is thought to be unoppressive, liberating, and calming: the very opposite of Catholic doctrine.

There can be no powerful evangelization unless we recover a sense of the mind-blowing liberation and beauty of our doctrine. Take the Trinity. For most Catholics, I suspect, it is celestial mathematics that has nothing to do with the ordinary challenges of living. I do not think that we have a hope in hell of sharing our faith unless we rediscover the dizzy excitement of believing, for example, in the divinity of Christ. Gregory of Nyssa famously wrote that "if in this city [Constantinople] you ask anyone for change, he will discuss with you whether the Son of man is begotten or unbegotten. If you ask about the quality of bread, you will receive the answer that 'the Father is greater, the Son is less.' If you suggest that a bath is desirable, you will be told that 'there was nothing before the Son was created.'"[5] Does this happen to you in Walmart? Does it happen in your communities? I have sometimes suggested to the brethren that a bath is desirable but never received a theological response!

Christianity is an intellectually demanding teaching. It makes you think. It pushes you beyond easy answers. Indeed it pushes you beyond any facile answers! Vincent McNabb used to say to the novices in the 1920s, "Think! Think of anything, but for God's sake, think." Brian Davies, OP, a Dominican teaching at Fordham, was once sitting on a bus and he overheard a conversation between two women in front of him. One recounted her terrible sufferings. The other said, "Well, my dear, you must be philosophical about it." "What does 'philosophical' mean?" "It means that you don't think about it." Our society has largely lost confidence in reasoning, which is one reason that it distrusts doctrine, since it does not know how to engage with it rationally. Christianity without doctrine would be like steak and kidney pie without the steak. Or as a character said in *Pride and Prejudice*, like a ball without the dancing.

We shall only have something to say in conversation with our contemporaries if we refuse to dumb down. We have two thousand years of rigorous praying and thinking about the deepest questions. We must be faithful to the complexity of things. I was once sitting next to a lay chaplain to a university in England. She was moaning about the bishops' statement on gay marriage. "They just reduced marriage to reproduction," she said. I replied that that was not fair. It was an intelligent and nuanced document. To which she replied, "I don't do nuance." Justice and truth demand nuance.

Doctrine keeps alive the drama of the Christian life. This is what Chesterton called "the adventure of orthodoxy." The young will not in the long run be drawn to a religion that is an innocuous spirituality: light a candle, feel good about yourself, and find where you are on the Enneagram. If we share with them the challenge to give up everything and follow Christ, they may run away in terror, but they might just find here the adventure for which they have always yearned. Christianity should carry a health warning. During a plane flight, I watched the popular *Game of Thrones*. It was rather silly. But people love it because it is a drama of love and death. If we do not offer our drama, which is the greatest there has ever been, people will settle for *Game of Thrones*.

Have you seen that extraordinary film *Of Gods and Men*? It is the story of a small community of Trappist monks living in the Atlas Mountains in Algeria in the 1990s. They get caught up in the rising tide of violence, trapped between the Islamist terrorists and the brutal Algerian army. Finally they come to accept that they must stay, even though this may cost them their lives. The youngest, Christophe, says to the prior, "But I did not become a monk to die." And the prior replies, "But you have already given away your life." On May 21, 1996, they were taken away in the night, and later their heads were found in plastic bags hanging from the trees under the monastery. I went to see this film in a cinema in Oxford, full of students and faculty. At the end there was complete silence. We waited to the end of the credits. No one wanted to go. One does not often find that at the end of a sermon.

Dorothy Sayers said, "The dogma is the drama—not beautiful phrases, nor comforting sentiments, nor vague aspirations to loving-kindness and uplift, nor the promise of something nice after death—but the terrifying assertion that the same God who made the world, lived in the world and passed through the grave and gate of death. Show that to the heathen, and they may not believe it, but at least they may realise that here is something that a man might be glad to believe."[6] Some Christians will not want to hear this. Michael Heher, a priest of the Orange diocese, wrote, "Congregants often want uplifting generalities and heart-warming comfort food and what we really need is someone like Flannery O'Connor who can shock us into seeing how hard and crucial discipleship is." The church will not keep alive for long on the theological equivalent of junk food.

I was a young friar in the late sixties. It was a time of crisis in my province. Lots of people left the Order. I stayed because theologians like Herbert McCabe showed us the beauty, the liberation of doctrine, which sustains our faith when the emotional excitement has burnt low, and when the Holy Spirit seems to have taken a break.

So this is what we bring to the conversation, our Christian doctrine, with all its intellectual rigor and dramatic vigor. But there will be no conversation unless we also come to learn. It was said of St. Dominic that he understood everything *"humili cordis intelligentia,"*[7] through the humble intelligence of his heart.

I went to Algeria a month after the murder of the monks, above all to see our brother Pierre Claverie, the bishop of Oran, who had received death threats. He said that in dialogue, "I have need of the truth of the other. I not only accept that the Other is Other, a distinct subject with freedom of conscience, but I accept that he or she may possess a part of the truth that I do not have, and without which my own search for the truth cannot be fully realized."[8] Pierre himself was murdered on August 1, 1996, with his young Muslim friend Mohamed Bouchikhi, who was driving him that day.

I cannot stress too strongly that dialogue here is not an alternative to evangelization. It is not about finding points in common, seeking the lowest common denominator. It has nothing to do with amiable fuzziness. At its truest, it is the conversation that makes our hearts burn within us; it is an encounter with the Lord, the stranger on the road. It is an experience of grace, *hilaritas*. Pierre Claverie asserted that conversation should always lead to conversion, and *my* conversion first of all. Sin, he said, "is the desire to make oneself the centre of the world, the desire to be oneself for oneself, on one's own terms, before others and before God, to see everything in terms of oneself."[9] So dialogue at its best is a liberating experience in which one is healed of egoism, initiated into new friendship, and led more deeply into the mystery of God's truth. This can be true even in dialogue with a convinced atheist; indeed there is no other way.

For this to happen, once again, two things are necessary: one must get out of one's depth, and discover new words together. At the beginning of the new millennium, John Paul II summoned us: *Duc in altum*. Row out into the depths. Lose your footing. We must have the courage to walk on the water like St. Peter, and not panic if we find ourselves sinking.

There is no evangelization, paradoxically, unless one is prepared to grapple with questions to which one does not know the answer. Cardinal Walter Kasper said that the church would have much more authority if she said more often, "I do not know." Let me quote the Israeli poet, Yehuda Amichai:

> The place where we are right
> is hard and trampled
> like a yard.
>
> But doubts and loves
> dig up the world
> like a mole, a plow.[10]

If we get out of our depth, then we shall have to beg for help from others, even people who do not share our faith. Saint Dominic wished his brethren to be beggars, and not just for bread. In admitting that we need their truth, then we may open them to accept ours. We shall have no authority unless we give authority to others.

So what are the areas in which we, the church, are rather at sea these days? Curiously, it is often around questions of gender and sexuality. This is *not* because sexuality is of itself of supreme moral importance. McCabe wrote, "So long as Christian morality is thought to be mainly about whether and when people should go to bed, no bishops are going to be crucified. And this, as I say, is depressing."[11] Not that we positively want our bishops to be crucified! But our society is in a real state of puzzlement about the nature of gender difference, the significance of being male and female. Here the church has an ancient and wise tradition, a Christian anthropology. But this needs to grow in dialogue with people in our society who puzzle over gender identity. We must attend to their experience and be drawn beyond our comfort zone, otherwise our theological tradition will wither. If there is no genetic moment, the tradition dies. Or think of homosexuality! Every mainline church is torn by the question. We are the heirs of a tradition of two millennia that appeared simply to deny any legitimate homosexual identity, and also we share a contemporary desire to welcome gay people in every way. The temptation is to sit silently and nod and wink suggestively! Watch my lips! But *Duc in altum*! Get into the conversation with gay people, listen and learn. Then we may have something to say. We may challenge the assumptions of our society, but we shall be heard.

Or think of reactions to the recent book by the French economist Thomas Piketty.[12] He has argued that our present model of capitalism is generating profound inequalities. It is tearing apart the human community, driving an ever deeper wedge between the rich and the poor. But what other economic models are there? Does the church dare to get involved in this fundamental question of economic justice and search with our contemporaries for a new economic vision? The church was deeply involved in debates at the beginning of modern capitalism, tackling the hard questions around usury. Will we be there now in the search for a new way forward as this model of capitalism nears its end?

Tom Beaudoin of Fordham University wrote, "We search for faith in the midst of profound theological, social, personal and sexual ambiguities."[13] We show our confidence in the Holy Spirit leading us into all truth precisely by daring to venture into ambiguities and not be quite sure where we will end up. Cardinal Richelieu warned us: "You abandon ambiguity at your peril."

Sometimes we must live with truths that seem to be in opposition to each other and that we cannot reconcile. For example, how do we reconcile supporting marriage and at the same time welcoming the divorced and remarried? We must be patient as we await the way forward. The truth is one in God, and until we are fully taken up into God, we must endure moments when truths seem to be incompatible. We may have little that we can say boldly. But that might be for the best. William Hill, OP, wrote, "God cannot do without the stammering ways in which we strive to give utterance to that Word."[14] Paradoxically such words may have more authority than those of preachers who are boiling over with conviction. Usually loud conviction is in inverse proportion to actual confidence.

Secondly, in any real conversation, you seek new words with the other. Sometimes you offer your words and sometimes you accept theirs, or coin fresh ones. Neither imposes a vocabulary on the other. Saint Augustine said, "We are urged to sing a new song to the Lord, as new people who have learned a new song. . . . The new human, the new song, the new covenant, all belong to the one kingdom of God, and so the new human will sing a new song and will belong to the new covenant."[15] On the road to Emmaus, the Lord taught disciples a new way of reading the Scriptures.

Pope Francis, in *Evangelii Gaudium*, sees this newness as an inherent dimension of evangelization. He quotes St. Irenaeus: " 'By his coming, Christ brought with him all newness.' . . . Every form of authentic evangelization is always 'new' "(11). This is Ernst's "genetic moment," as we edge our way into ways of speaking that have a tiny share in the fresh spaciousness of God's word, a word that we are always at the beginning of learning to speak.

T. S. Eliot in "Little Gidding" wrote,

> Last season's fruit is eaten
> And the fulfilled beast shall kick the empty pail.
> For last year's words belong to last year's language
> And next year's words await another voice.[16]

So conversations on the road may set our hearts burning. But how can we live fruitfully the tensions between doctrine and doubting, and confidence and humility? What sustains us as we stammer? I will conclude in mentioning just two ways in which we carry on walking even when, like cartoon characters who have walked off the end of a cliff, we are suspended over the void.

The disciples are filled with joy as he talks to them on the road. But it is only at Emmaus when he breaks the bread that their eyes are opened. It is what he *did* that makes sense of what they felt in a muddled way, their inexplicable joy. Gestures often point toward an intuitive resolution of tensions that we cannot as yet articulate. It was only in this gesture that the necessity of his death is reconciled with his freedom as the Son of God. Paul VI startled the world by taking off his episcopal ring and placing it on the finger of Michael Ramsey, the archbishop of Canterbury. What did this mean? What did it say about Anglican orders? It symbolized a unity to which they aspired and already in some sense had, even if they could not see how to make sense of it. Gestures can be sacramental of a truth that we cannot yet get our heads around.

Pope Francis speaks so powerfully, even to people who do not believe, because of his gestures: he washes the feet of young prisoners on Maundy

Thursday, including a Muslim girl. That is a gesture that is pregnant with all sorts of meanings that we cannot as yet digest. He hugs a man covered with disfiguring boils; he goes to celebrate Mass at Lampedusa where so many immigrants perished at sea.

Finally, a brief word on beauty. In his keynote address on evangelization to the Los Angeles Religious Education Congress this year, Robert Barron put beauty first. People fear that doctrine is doctrinaire, and that a moral vision is moralistic. Beauty has its own authority that draws us without threatening our freedom. The beautiful will lure us toward the true and the good. This was certainly so for the Orkney poet George Mackay Brown. His biographer, Ron Ferguson, wrote that "beauty and literature hooked him and reeled him in. It was what he saw as the beauty of the Christian doctrines of the Incarnation and Christ's Passion which made him a believer. *Nowhere in all created literature, not in Homer, Dante, Shakespeare, Goethe, is there anything of such awesome majesty and power as the drama of the Passion. The imagination could never compass that—it* must *be true.*"[17]

Beauty, like gestures, often points toward a spacious truth for which we do not yet have the words. Sarah Coakley wrote a book on the relationship between theology, prayer, gender, and art. It attempts to recover the primal unity of all Christian living and thinking. For me, the most fascinating chapter is on the iconography of the Trinity. Most representations of this doctrine are either tritheistic, with three similar figures standing beside each other, or Arian, with the Father clearly the boss. How could you have a representation of this mystery? But the most successful, she writes, "do not attempt to *describe* what it is like *chez God*, but rather stir imagination, or direct the will, beyond the known towards the unknown, prompting symbolic 'hints half guessed.'"[18] As Paul Ricoeur said, "The symbol gives rise to thought."[19] Coakley's examples range from a dynamic sixteenth-century image of three hares engaged in a wild dance to an almost abstract swirling image painted by Marlene Scholz, a former Dominican sister. Art can sustain the conversation when we have not yet found words on which to agree.

So evangelization happens in our conversation with strangers. We communicate in the grace-filled event. We should boldly share our doctrine and humbly learn. We must dare to get out of our depth, be forced to swim and beg the help of our interlocutors. We shall experience the *hilaritas* of God's grace and discover his presence in friendship.

Endnotes

1. Anthony Trollope, *Barchester Towers* (London: Dodd, Mead & Co., 1904), Chapter VI, "War."

2. Cornelius Ernst, *The Theology of Grace*, Theology Today series, vol. 17 (Dublin: Fides, 1974), 74.

3. James Alison, *Undergoing God: Dispatches from the Scene of a Break-In* (London: Darton, Longman and Todd, 2006), 35–36.

4. G. K. Chesterton, "The Mercy of Mr. Arnold Bennett," in *Fancies vs. Fads* (London: Methuen and Co., 1923).

5. Quoted by W. H. C. Frend, *The Early Church* (Philadelphia: Fortress, 1982), 174.

6. Dorothy L. Sayers, *The Whimsical Christian: 18 Essays* (New York: Macmillan, 1978), 27.

7. Jordan of Saxony, *Libellus* 7.

8. Jean-Jacques Pérennès, *A Life Poured Out: Pierre Claverie of Algeria* (Maryknoll, NY: Orbis, 2007), 148.

9. Ibid., 214.

10. Yehuda Amichai, "The Place Where We Are Right," in *The Selected Poetry of Yehuda Amichai*, ed. and trans. Chana Bloch and Stephen Mitchell (Berkeley: University of California Press, 2013).

11. Herbert McCabe, *Law, Love and Language* (London: Sheed & Ward, 1968), 164.

12. Thomas Piketty, *Capital in the Twenty-First Century* (Cambridge, MA: Belknap Press of Harvard University Press, 2014).

13. Tom Beaudoin, *Virtual Faith: The Irreverent Spiritual Quest of Generation X* (San Francisco: Jossey-Bass, 1998), 122.

14. William Hill, "Preaching as a 'Moment' in Theology," in *Search for the Absent God: Tradition and Modernity in Religious Understanding* (New York: Crossroad, 1992), 186.

15. Sermo 34.1–3, 5–6; CCL 41, 424–26.

16. "Four Quartets," *The Complete Poems and Plays of T. S. Eliot* (London: Faber, 1969), 194.

17. Ron Ferguson, *George Mackay Brown: The Wound and the Gift* (Edinburgh: Saint Andrew Press, 2011), 139.

18. Sarah Coakley, *God, Sexuality, and the Self: An Essay 'On the Trinity'* (Cambridge, UK: Cambridge University Press, 2013), 197.

19. Paul Ricoeur, *The Symbolism of Evil* (Boston: Beacon Press, 1967), 347–57.

Chapter 2

La Virgen de Guadalupe as Mother and Master Icon for the New Evangelization

Virgilio Elizondo

Ever since early childhood I can remember with very fond memories the great celebrations in our parish around the feast of Our Lady of Guadalupe. We would get up early in the morning before dawn to greet her with songs and dances. I had never heard of Easter sunrise services, but this was a sunrise service for me; it celebrated the beginning of a new day. When I was around seven or eight years old we went on pilgrimage to the shrine in Mexico City. While walking through the crowded doors of the basilica and being pushed by mobs of fellow pilgrims, all of a sudden we saw her image as if she was coming to us. It was a fascinating, incredible experience.

I have had many testimonies of her power throughout my fifty-one years as a priest. I remember giving a workshop to Spanish-speaking parishioners in Seattle. The pastor asked if I would mind speaking to the English-speaking parishioners about Our Lady since he had installed her image but they knew little about her. One evening I gave my most basic talk about Guadalupe. At the end, a couple with four or five children came up to me to offer their testimony. He spoke first, telling me how they had been in a horrible accident; they had been broadsided and his wife had been hit very badly and had gone into a coma. Then she spoke: "Yes, I blacked out. In my unconsciousness, I saw Our Lady of Guadalupe come to me, sat by me and told me to get up, my family needed me. At that moment I came out of the coma and have been telling the story ever since."

Another time, at the beginning of the first Iraq war, a military couple came to me and asked if I would bless their Our Lady of Guadalupe tattoos. Never having blessed a tattoo before, I asked them if they would like to have a medal, holy card, or rosary. They looked at me with eyes that said, "How stupid can you be!" and went on to explain. "Father, we are going to war. We might lose those objects, but we would not lose the tattoo—she would be on our bodies." I blessed my first tattoo.

Most Successful Evangelization since Pentecost

The story begins in 1531 among the most marginalized and subjugated people living on the peripheries of the great imperial capital of Mexico. From that locale her devotion has spread to the entire world. She appears in churches and chapels throughout the American continents. I remember walking into a church in Nagasaki and immediately running into an image of Guadalupe. I've seen her in Jerusalem, in Paris, in New York City, in Quebec, in Prague, and other places. She has gone from being condemned by the early missioners to being acclaimed universally and crowned as empress and mother of America by the popes. John Paul II proclaimed her as the star of the first and new evangelization.

She has deeply penetrated entire cultures, reaching into the hearts of people. She is present in works of art, music, TV programs, movies, plays, and even operas. Towns, parks, neighborhoods, and even persons are named after her. She is tattooed on the bodies of many persons, songs and poems are composed in her honor, and she appears even in bars, buses, restaurants, beauty salons, cars, planes, and so on.

She was the battle cry of the leaders of Mexico's independence movement led by Fr. Miguel Hidalgo and in our own times was the standard-bearer of the struggle for justice and humane treatment of farmworkers led by Cesar Chavez. She has been a source of strength for people's struggles for liberation.

Her evangelizing power can best be seen in the religious expressions of the people. She is the ever-present loving and protecting mother of the people. There are many popular religious practices, feasts, processions, pilgrimages, hymns, novenas, medals, theological works, and sermons. Religious communities bear her name as well as churches and shrines.

Our Lady of Guadalupe has been most important in the lives of people precisely because she is not a dogma that has to be believed, but a gift of God's merciful love that is experienced by everyone. Because she is not necessary, she is such a precious and tender gift full of possibilities for theological reflection.

Pope John Paul II declared, "In the prayer composed for the Special Assembly for America of the Synod of Bishops, Holy Mary of Guadalupe is invoked as 'Patroness of all America and Star of the first and new evangelization.' In view of this, I welcome with joy the proposal of the Synod Fathers that the feast of Our Lady of Guadalupe, Mother and Evangelizer of America, be celebrated throughout the continent on December 12."[1]

Narrative and Icon: Crisis and Crucifixion

The apparitions took place in 1531, just ten years after the conquest. This was probably the most brutal and difficult time for the native peoples. Their entire world had come to an end. Nothing made sense anymore. They had passed from being a proud people with a well-ordered way of life to being completely subjugated. You might well say that this was the time of a collective crucifixion of the people. They had been totally conquered—a totally new way of life, new dress, new foods, new customs, new language. Their temples had been destroyed, their warriors had been killed, their women had been raped, and now they were told their gods were not true. Their whole world of meaning had been destroyed, so why live? They only wanted to die.

The Native Worldview

To fully appreciate the impact of Our Lady of Guadalupe it is important to take a brief look at the native worldview of the people of Mexico. Very different from our Western concept of right or wrong, either/or is the concept of duality whereby everything is both/and. For example, there is beauty in ugliness and ugliness in beauty, light in darkness and darkness in light, joy in sadness and sadness in joy, life in death and death in life, male in the female and female in the male. Thus reality could best be expressed poetically in two visual concepts. For example, a person would be countenance and heart. Divine truth would be beauty that can be seen and heard, as in flower and song. Supreme truth could be expressed poetically since a poem opens the imagination to the beyond. They were a very philosophical and literary people, but they were poetic and picto-graphic, not logical and alphabetical. Their temples were not only the physical centers of life but they were equally symbolic of their entire way of life. Into this world came the conquistadores trying to destroy every-thing native as they tried to build up New Spain, and the missioners trying to proclaim the Gospel and establish the kingdom of God.

Efforts at Evangelization

By the early 1500s there was in Spain a vibrant renewal program of the church led by Cardinal Francisco Ximenes de Cisneros that insisted on a return to the Scriptures and the origins of the church. The earliest mission-ers came from the school of biblical renewal of Alcala. The discovery of the vast lands previously unknown and unsuspected gave rise to much theo-logical speculation. Many saw the discovery of new lands as the fulfillment of the prophecies of Joachim de Fiore, who had divided the world into three periods: the age of the Father that was the period of the law; the period of the Son, which would be the period of the church; and finally the period of the Spirit, when the world would be a large community led by spiritual men with an emphasis on evangelical poverty.

The first Franciscan missioners who came to Mexico were twelve in number. They were the new apostolic college that came to begin the new church that would be free of all the excesses and abuses of the church of Europe. Soon twelve Dominicans would also come to the New World to continue the work of building the new church of the spirit. They were all men of great virtue, practicing radical poverty, and creative theologians. They came with a well-prepared program of evangelization according to their worldview, not realizing that it would not make sense to a completely different worldview. The native theologians of Mexico politely demolished their best efforts. At the rational level, they encountered a complete block-age due to a totally different philosophical and linguistic base and most of all due to the scandal of the so-called Christian Spaniards.

The great missioners seemed to have failed, but a simple Franciscan lay brother, Pedro de Gante, would be the great evangelizer of Mexico. It was said that he spent the first few years playing with the children so as to be totally reborn into ancient Mexico. He quickly discovered that the natives expressed themselves through art and the use of beautiful native dyes. He arranged to bring in Flemish painters to begin the great tradition of Mexican art. Knowing that the natives communicated about

God through poetry and song, he adapted the native melodies to have a catechetical message. Acknowledging their sense of beauty, he helped in the building of beautiful temples—they were to be the most beautiful buildings of the town, for beauty attracts, and they were to be decorated with beautiful murals depicting various biblical scenes. Finally, knowing the natives' sense of collective ritual, he organized various biblical dramas in which the people would be active participants. He did not condemn human sacrifice but made it known that now it was no longer necessary because the man-God, Jesus of Nazareth, has already been crucified for all of us. Crosses were placed upon the altars of sacrifice to indicate the one sacrifice surpassed all their previous ones.

It was a holistic evangelization that reached into the depths of the collective heart of the people. He evangelized people by appealing to every level of their entire culture. However, all these good efforts seemed to be useless because there were very few converts. The memory and the scandals of the conquest were too recent for the people to be able to understand the message of the Gospel of love, forgiveness, and mercy. Their hard work would lay the foundations for a deeply inculturated evangelization. The missioners prayed and prayed for some kind of a signal, for some divine intervention, and their prayers would be answered in 1531 in a totally unsuspected and unimagined way.

The Unsuspected Event: The Great Synthesis

We don't know exactly what happened. There were no video cameras around to record the event, but we do have the poetic memory. For ancient peoples, oral tradition was very sacred and credible. The people remembered and passed it on to the next generation. In time the elements of the story were placed together into the poetic memory as we have it today.

"While it was still dark" on December 9, 1531, Juan Diego was on his way to Tlatelolco to learn about the things of God. The dark night refers to several things. It refers to the condition of the people for whom nothing made sense anymore, the times of total desolation, when even their gods seemed to have abandoned them, but it also refers to the final moments before creation when the gods were making their final deliberations. As he went by Tepeyac it was "beginning to dawn." The expression was often used in Nahua mythology to indicate final moments when new creation had begun, when the first buds of new life were coming into existence. Juan Diego is thus placed at a moment of creation. He is attracted by the "beautiful singing of the birds." Beautiful music indicated the beginning of a divine communication while the birds were messengers of God.

He goes to the source of the music at the top of the hill, like a native priest going to the top of a pyramid but not to offer human sacrifice. There he meets a beautiful lady that radiates the sun, like their sun god who was the source of life, and calls him by name in a very endearing way. He is not terrified in any way. He feels good in her presence. He is affirmed as a human being. The lady identifies herself as Holy Mary, Mother of God and the mother of all the gods—both Spaniard and Nahua. It's a terrific interreligious introduction.

She tells him that he is to go to the bishop and tell him that he is to construct a temple where she can remedy all their ills and show all her love, mercy, and compassion to all the inhabitants of this land. Sounds simple enough, but when you see the symbolic meaning there is much more. The natives were to listen and obey, but now a native is told to go to the chief authority in the center of the city and tell him to come out to the periphery and build a temple! The reversal is clear: the bishop is to be the listener and he is to go from the center to the periphery where the people are. God speaks through the poor, simple, and marginal.

In the audience with the bishop it is Juan Diego who identifies her as the Mother of our Lord and Savior Jesus Christ. Naturally the bishop is skeptical. He asks questions. Juan Diego feels totally rejected because he thinks that he has failed the Lady. He now believes all the lies that the Spaniards were saying about the natives. He feels totally unworthy and completely useless. He asks the Lady to send someone else, someone important, dignified, and credible. But the Lady insists that he is to be her trusted messenger. She will give him a sign for the bishop to believe. Juan Diego hesitates because his uncle is dying. But the Lady assures him that he will not die of the present disease. She tells him to go to the top of the mountain and there he will find beautiful flowers from Castile. December was not the season for flowers and Tepeyac was not a place for them either. Juan Diego goes to the top and finds beautiful flowers from Castile. He cuts them, puts them in his mantle, and goes off to the bishop. He is so happy and confident that he will be believed. Out of the native soil of Mexico flowers from Spain blossomed. The missioners had brought the Gospel and planted deeply into the native soil. Now the faith would begin to blossom! A beautiful poetic way of saying the Gospel had been implanted, had been inculturated.

Juan Diego carries the beautiful flowers from Castile to the bishop, never suspecting that what he carries is far greater than the flowers he had found at Tepeyac. As he unrolls his mantle in the presence of the bishop, the beautiful image of Our Lady of Guadalupe appears on the mantle and has been there since December 12, 1531. The bishop and all his attendants kneel and ask for forgiveness for not having believed and later on go out to Tepeyac to begin the construction of her temple, the new church among the poor of the periphery. Juan Diego is converted from a silent to a speaking Indian while the bishop is converted from a teaching to a listening bishop, and together they will build the new church of the Americas. I am convinced that the temple Guadalupe asked for has not yet been built. It is the temple of an America without borders, a land for all the peoples of the world, where all can be her beloved children.

The narrative had begun with the beautiful singing of the birds and had come to completion with the beautiful flowers from Castile, a marvelous way of saying "word of God." In the context of this divine revelation, the image of Our Lady appeared painted on the mantle of Juan Diego. This marks the birth of the new church of the Americas, born out of the womb of the native soil impregnated by the word of God.

The Message in the Image

It is important to remember that the natives were a pictographic people who communicated through symbolic expressions. Every detail of the image of Our Lady has a beautiful and profound meaning for those who can read the code. Let me make a brief attempt.

Clouds cover the entire mantle, so it is a heavenly manifestation. She is surrounded by the sun, the principal manifestation of God for the Nahua—they were known as the people of the sun—so she tells the people she is greater than their sun god but she does not destroy the sun. This is a very important detail, for at this time the missioners were attempting to destroy all the native symbols of God. She does not destroy the principal religious symbol; she merely transcends it. She equally does not destroy the moon goddess, but she is greater.

She appears as both virgin and mother. Her hair is parted down the middle like that of a young virgin and she wears the band of maternity. She is divine because she is covered with the blue-green mantle, a color reserved for divinity, while she is very earthy because she is dressed with the soft, brownish-pink color of the earth. She unites heaven and earth. Yet she is not a goddess, for she has a tender and compassionate face with eyes that see. Many have studied her eyes and claim they see the image of Juan Diego in the pupil of her eye. I personally believe that the image one sees in her eye is that of the person looking at her. Her hands are in a position of offering herself to the people. Her knee is slightly bent, for the natives believed that it was through dance that you entered into communion with the gods. She is in a position of dance, leading the people in their dance with God. Finally, right over her belly, one finds the figure of the four-leaf clover that was the symbol for the present age of the fifth sun. She carries within her womb the beginning of the new era—the age of the spirit!

Interpretation

The entire narrative is not only presented as a divine manifestation (song and flower) but the imagery that it uses is that of a creation or resurrection account. It is the story of a new beginning, or as stated in the Plaza of the Three Cultures outside Mexico City, "Neither a defeat nor a victory, but the painful birth of the *mestizo* people that is Mexico today."

At a time when the human dignity of the conquered people was being trampled upon and crushed, and it was even questioned whether they were human or natural slaves, the Lady is very respectful in dealing with Juan Diego, calling him by name and making him her trusted messenger, giving a voice to the silenced native, giving a voice to the poor, the excluded, the marginalized. There is nothing more painful and dehumanizing than treating persons like anonymous things, treating them like dogs or animals. Calling someone by name is recognizing and affirming their humanity. Guadalupe recognizes and affirms the basic human dignity of the crushed native. She converses with him as an equal, recognizes his situation as being that of a poor man but assures him of his basic human dignity. In her presence, Juan Diego is not a conquered native but a free and dignified human being, joyful and full of confidence.

There are no threats of punishment, hell, or damnation in the encounter, but simply an invitation to help her in her project to build a temple wherein she can show all her love, mercy, and affection. The narrative and image bring out the truth, goodness, and beauty of both cultures, while transforming them by cleaning them of their negative elements—the natives of the need for human sacrifice and the Catholicism of the Iberians with its emphasis on a punishing God. The God of Guadalupe is a God of mercy and love. Guadalupe would be transformative of both cultures as it would call both to a deep conversion that would bring out new possibilities of both, new beauty, new imagery, and a new meaning of life together. One culture would not have to destroy the other and the other culture would not have to completely resist, but both would form something new. Out of the ashes of the old, something new would erupt, a new Christian culture. The mestizo image of Guadalupe incorporates the new mestizo culture that was just beginning into the universal family of the children of God. They are now incorporated into the Catholic community, making it ever more catholic—for catholicity is the unity in diversity of the diverse people of the planet.

The entire account is very respectful of the cultural anthropology of the native people while carefully and very delicately bringing in the essential elements of the Gospel. It is really the Gospel presented in native terms. All of the elements of a true inculturated evangelization are carefully, beautifully, and poetically presented in the Guadalupe narrative and image. The people who had just wanted to die now began to live; they began to sing their songs and take part in their festivals.

Guadalupe and the New Evangelization

We have much to learn from the Guadalupe narrative and image. If we are to be a "poor church for the poor," can we listen to the voices of the poor, the marginalized, the immigrant, the foreigner, the beggar, the despised and enter into solidarity with them in building the church among them? Can we listen to the voices of the thousands of refugee children who are coming across the border fleeing from violence and certain death? This is one of our most immediate challenges today. Are we as a nation sending thousands of children back to be murdered simply because they are brown, poor, and defenseless?

What would it mean for us to be culturally respectful in our growing multicultural society yet culturally transformative of everyone? The key to this is love. Love leads us to understanding and understanding increases our love. Love opens up the imagination to new possibilities. How can we initiate and carry on a conversation that might lead to an encounter with the Lord and conversion? Guadalupe was not just an event but it was the beginning of a movement, a conversation, a way of life that invites people to a personal encounter and conversion.

And what sort of icon could convey the kind of unique integrative power that Guadalupe exercised over the Mesoamerican collective imagination? Our continent is becoming more and more multicultural as different peoples come in from various parts of the world. The real meaning of the "new world" is that it is a home for all the peoples of the world. Tolerance for difference, tolerance for the "other" is something totally foreign to many around the world. Yet we are called to make our continent—the New World—a place for all the peoples of the world where tolerance is just the first step in building a community of friends. We have a long way to go, but we have started the process.

I am convinced that it is in the memory of the events surrounding Our Lady of Guadalupe at the beginning of the New World that we will find the key to our task. As the bishops of the continent asked St. John Paul II to name her "Patroness of all America and Star of the first and new evangelization"—she opened the doors to evangelization and will be the star leading us into the New Evangelization today.[2]

Endnotes

1. John Paul II, *Ecclesia in America* 11, http://w2.vatican.va/content/john-paul-ii/en/apost_exhortations/documents/hf_jp-ii_exh_22011999_ecclesia-in-america.html.

2. In *Evangelii Gaudium* 287–88, Pope Francis refers to Mary as the "star of the new evangelization."

Chapter 3

Forming Preachers
for the New Evangelization

Honora Werner, OP

This topic, forming preachers for the New Evangelization, did not immediately appeal to my imagination. But as I have pondered this, I am really enthusiastic. Why? Partly because I am baptized and partly because I am a Dominican who teaches homiletics and have had experience in the formation of seminarians!

As Catholics we are not accustomed to speaking of ourselves as evangelizers, never mind doing the work! People who go to foreign lands—maybe. But not us stay-at-home types. Yet, all are commissioned as preachers by baptism—not just the clerics! Access to our many pulpits is limited because of the realities of our lives. But we must ask, "What are *our* pulpits?" Personally each of us must ask, "What is *my* pulpit? Are there more than one for me?" Then, we must, as my friend Ann Willits proclaims, "Occupy those pulpits!" Some are liturgical. Most are not!

The church calls us to evangelization by her very nature. In his apostolic exhortation *Evangelii Gaudium*, Pope Francis calls the church a missionary disciple (40), a community of missionary disciples and an evangelizing community (24). Why is the church? What is her reason for being? The essential mission of the church, indeed her deepest identity, is "the task of evangelizing all people."[1]

What is our role in the church? Conservation of the truths we have received through tradition? Or missionary activity beyond our parish boundaries, and perhaps even beyond our comfort zones? We are a church with the commission from Jesus to proclaim the Good News to all the world! So missionary it is! Conserving the truths serves the mission!

We will consider formation of preachers for the New Evangelization in three steps:

1. *Forming ourselves*
2. *Forming our students*
3. *Forming the people of God (our assemblies)*

Evangelii Gaudium provides a "manual" for any who will evangelize. Deacon Devon Wolfe offers a four-word practical guide, a program for all evangelizers:

Prayer   Care   Share   Dare[2]

Forming Ourselves

We are far from dead, so we are works in progress. Being formed—even though seminary and novitiate were years ago—is present progressive tense! We cannot give what we do not have. So in order to proclaim the goodness of God, the Gospel of Jesus, we need regular daily encounters with Christ, with God. *Prayer*, especially *lectio* with the Lectionary readings of the day, Eucharist, and reconciliation are essential to our ongoing formation program. Those close encounters through Word and sacrament shape our thinking and perceptions. We meet the God whose Good News we are called to proclaim. Biblical characters encountered God in one way or another, and as we pray with them, we realize, that like them, we meet the same God—or we avoid such a meeting! The Eucharist reminds us of the paschal pattern of all life, from the first creatures billions of years ago, until now. They live, they die, and in their deaths, new life is born. Jesus lived that pattern for decades, dying to various phases of life, various relationships, even homes, finally dying to his own life on the cross, and then he was raised to new life on Easter. He lived the pattern deliberately and willingly. We humans can choose to do that or to resist it at every turn, ultimately succumbing to it anyway! Other creatures do not have that choice. They live it "automatically." As we encounter Jesus in the Eucharist and celebrate that paschal mystery, we are inspired, strengthened, and nourished to live out our own paschal pattern of life, death, new life. Reconciliation allows us to experience God's mercy and, in turn, become ministers of reconciliation with others, as Paul calls us to be in 2 Corinthians 5:18.

The *care* part of the process may seem obvious. But there are issues that we all can recognize and perhaps address. Evangelizers need to know the people to whom they proclaim the Gospel. Otherwise, how can they love them? In recognizing persons in need of evangelization, we ask, "Who among us has yet to hear the Good News?" Some "cradle Catholics" are among those people. Why can they not hear? Are they deafened by the crass voices in the culture? deafened by the cold, seemingly unfeeling affect of preachers and pastoral ministers they have encountered? deafened by being rejected because of some condition of their lives—a disability, an ethnic identity, a sexual orientation, gender itself? The list can go on and on, but many conditions cause them to be hard of hearing toward the Gospel. Once we realize that they cannot hear us, what can we do about it?

What does our hospitality look like from the outside? For example, does the parish bulletin—describing us as welcoming, open to all who come, and so on—match the reality? When people call the church, does the one answering the phone sometimes give an impression that is opposite the lovely language of the mission statement? Or upon trying to visit the church, people may find signs proclaiming all are welcome, but there is no indication of the way a person in a wheelchair could come in. Miss Reilly in sixth grade (paraphrasing Ralph Waldo Emerson) often said to us, "Who you are and what you do speaks so loudly that I cannot hear what you say!" What does our manner of greeting people say? "Come, I'd love to chat with you." "I'm too busy right now; some other time." "I have a headache; leave me alone, will ya?" Eucharistic people are characterized by hospitality, according to St. Paul.

Knowing and loving the Head is not enough! An evangelizer needs to know and love the members of the Body as well, not only the ones at Mass who hear them preach but the vast majority who do not celebrate with us at Mass. We meet them where they are. Pope Francis counsels us to take the Gospel outside to the streets—not to keep it locked in church buildings! We listen to their joys and hopes, sorrows and frustrations, anxieties and fears. We are all poor and afflicted in some way, so to listen to stories of others is to offer a sounding board that is credible. God has done this in the incarnation—sending the Second Person to live like us. God loves in us what God loves in Jesus! As children of this God, is our vision anything like that? Do we know the context we minister in, through its sports, art, pop culture, news, and so on? This is the work and the vision of hospitality, which is at the heart of evangelization. Hospitality invites all without exception—even the one offering it—to conversion and holiness.[3] Some will not accept this hospitality, but that is not the responsibility of the evangelizer. This is a demanding vocation and there are times when we simply do not feel up to it. Jesus was not always up for a visit with people. He was tired and hungry at times too. But he was able to work though those limits of his humanity to allow encounters with the children, the Samaritan woman at the well, and after a day of preaching to and feeding thousands, the obtuse disciples in the boat! I can hear you saying, "Yes, but he is God!" Right. But in imitation of him, we try.

We look deeply into the lives of our people to see evidence of God at work there. We may hear it, see it, feel it—but when we are perceptive, we will recognize it. Charity, joy, peace, patience, kindness, love, chastity, long-suffering—all the fruits of the Holy Spirit give evidence of God at work in a person or situation. We preachers need to be attuned to that holy presence and proclaim it.

Now we turn to the *share* part of the guide. What do we share? What message comes across the top of our pulpit? God's loving presence in our lives? God's endless mercy and forgiveness? For *everyone*? There is no sin that is greater than God's power of loving mercy. This is what Jesus preached. Some worry that this type of message condones all sorts of aberrant behavior. "Unless they fear God's punishment they will not behave! What we need in the church today is more preaching about sin." Is this good news? Is this Jesus' message? When he met people who had sinned publicly, did he condemn them right then and there? He showed mercy— and then "Go and sin no more." Hypocrisy was the only sin that had him go on the attack. But even that was after he had spent days, weeks, even months, trying to lure them into the embrace of his loving Father!

Another pulpit from which we share the Good News is working for justice. We are surrounded with evidence of injustice. The cries of the poor reach our ears daily, via media if not in person. So we roll up our sleeves and get to work. Such action gives credibility to the words we preach in the church pulpit.

In the process of working for justice we can be blinded by the evil we experience. So then, what do we share? The absence of God from the lives of faithful people? Or the very presence of God that they may not recognize, but that we do? And when we are outside the church building, in our other pulpits, do we simply decry the evil we see, or are we able to name traces of God present? We proclaim the *joy* of the Gospel!

As Catholic preachers, we are conscious of evil—injustice, oppression, disrespect of people, disregard of Earth—and certainly we can name those traces of God's "absence," but who will hear if that is all we proclaim? We can take a page from the playbook of advertising geniuses, who make the product nearly irresistible to us. Making God's presence clear so people can embrace it strengthens them and us in our struggle against evil. Without that strength, we will find the struggle hopeless.

Perhaps one of our pulpits is nearly wordless; it is the pulpit of service to those in need. Although most Catholics do not identify themselves as evangelists, they do cite work for justice, efforts to alleviate the suffering of people made poor, among our identifying characteristics, right up there with Eucharist and honoring the Mother of God, according to recent polls. At Vanderbilt University the Catholic community used to be known for its participation in and leadership of various organizations that served people in need. When one student was named head of the Oxfam Fast on campus, people said, "Gee, Denny, we didn't know you were Catholic!" Actually, he wasn't, but he delighted in sharing that with us campus ministers! The works of mercy and justice are an indispensable pulpit for Catholic evangelization. We need to find ourselves in them on a regular basis. In our verbal preaching from the liturgical pulpit, we need to name them consciously as evangelization. Catholic Relief Services, the Catholic Campaign for Human Development, and Catholic Charities are among the most effective organizations in the world. All are amazing pulpits! Please name them as evangelizers.

Peter Vaghi remarks that we live our lives on the road to Jericho. In Luke 10 the parable of the two men on that road depicts two neighbors, one in need, one able to help. At times we are all one or the other. Citing Matthew 25, Vaghi goes on to say that *Jesus* is the one needing mercy![4] "Go and do likewise" is a command to evangelize from the pulpit of the road to Jericho.

The final part of the guide to evangelization is *dare*. Since Catholics tend to think of evangelization as a basically Protestant activity, or as something done by people who are missionaries in foreign lands, moving us to see ourselves as evangelists takes a strong push. Yes, it takes courage. What if they tell me to be quiet? Supposing they laugh at me or mock me? What if I say the wrong thing? The excuses and reasons for our timidity are legion. A few years ago, I was serving as liturgist for a conference being held at Emory University. Reverend Andrew Young (former colleague of Dr. Martin Luther King Jr., later US ambassador to the United Nations, and mayor of Atlanta) was the preacher for that day's morning prayer. I busied myself in the sacristy, but he paced the floor, wringing his hands and muttering. I asked if there was anything he needed. He stopped and declared, "Andrew, if God can use the jaw-bone of an ass, he can sure use you!" Amen!

Dare to show that we are people who pray, people with real convictions based on our faith in Jesus. Our work, our ministry is not an annoying part of the week leading up to our day off. No, evangelization *is* our identity![5]

When our people hear our enthusiasm for evangelization in our references to daily events and circumstances, some of their fear may be allayed. We've got a good thing here, in this faith of ours. Surely our church is not a perfect society, but the richness and depth of the wisdom it carries from age to age is a treasure not meant for us alone. We cannot be in every pulpit out there. So it is up to us to help motivate those who do occupy those pulpits. When we stand in the liturgical pulpit we are role models for them as evangelizers. Our lives lend credibility to our words. Our words arise from our perception of God at work among our people. This is the same God whose stories we read from Scripture at every Mass. So when we make the connections for people, they are energized by the optimism, the grace, the realization that God *is* with them as has been promised from the very beginning.

Forming Our Students

First, let's be careful about what students think the church is. Use the papal documents to help them see that the essential nature of the church is evangelical and we are its ministers!

Of course, the formation of preachers for evangelization means teaching them how to *pray* daily, using *lectio divina*. How can they proclaim him whom they do not know? Participating in Eucharist and reconciliation are essentials as well, for the same reasons that they are for us, the teachers. Our students tend to be devout, but devotions cannot take the place of the Scripture and sacraments.

How can we form preachers who know and love the folks, preachers who *care*? The care part of the program for our students may involve revisiting Emily Post or an etiquette course! The simple act of writing thank-you notes is foreign to so many of them. Yet we are eucharistic people. So, of course, we say/write "thank you!" Imagine how the people would listen on Sunday if on Wednesday there had been a thank-you note in their mailbox from the preacher. Encourage the students to meet and get to know the back stories of the people in their lives, in their schools. Be sure they spend time outside the hallowed walls of the seminary and church buildings and meet the folks on the streets, literally.

How can we form our students as preachers—as people who *share* the Good News—when they are woefully ignorant of the traditions of the church? How can they explain what a certain custom or belief means if they do not know it themselves? So training in the basics of the faith and Catholic culture is essential for our students. Many come to the seminary with graduate degrees in engineering, the sciences, and even the humanities. But they are without the knowledge other generations learned "by heart" as children—from the family, the community, the schools. As novices, over fifty years ago, we had to memorize the *Baltimore Catechism*, no. 3. That was required for profession, a part of our formation. Theology studied from the *Summa* was done in our college classes. The *Summa* and the Catechism went hand in hand. Of course, we had to explain what we memorized in our own words. Thus, we were prepared to pass that information on to the children we would be teaching in a couple of years, in words we and they could understand. I don't know how this can be done in today's formation programs, but neglecting it is a mistake.

If we are teaching preaching, we need to check carefully the messages being preached by our students. Look at their focus, function, and doctrine statements. Do they add up to Good News? Note attitudes among the students that attract or repel. These surface in peer critiques of preaching, but also in casual conversations. Listen for them and address them.

Taking Pope Francis's letter as a guide, talk about the obstacles and challenges evangelizers face. This may help them *dare* to evangelize. Chapter 2 in *Evangelii Gaudium* is direct and practical in addressing issues like exclusion, the idolatry of money, cultural issues, selfishness and laziness, pessimism, worldliness—even spiritual worldliness—divisions among ourselves, sexism, ageism, dearth of religious and priestly vocations, to name a few. We dare not shy away from them. In fact, this chapter offers us and our students a sort of examen, worthy of days of reflection and retreat.

Forming the People of God

Then we come to the rest of the church as evangelizers, the ones who meet the people we never see or hear. Bruno Cadoré, OP, master of the Order of Preachers, wrote to the members of the Order urging them to recognize the importance of lay members' charism of preaching: "It is in [the] diversity of concrete situations in which lay people live that the questions are raised regarding the life of couples, the upbringing of children, professional responsibility, precarious employment, the financial level of living, and political or social commitment. It is also in the concreteness of experience that the death of a spouse or an offspring is felt, the stages of the journey to retirement, having to take professional redirection, the handicaps of advanced age."[6] Here the laity make an unparalleled contribution to understanding the word of God in real life. How can we ignore this vast army of evangelizers, this "community of missionary disciples," as Pope Francis names us?

First, teach people to *pray*, especially using *lectio divina*. Reading the Word and reflecting on it offers them (and us) the opportunity to encounter God and recognize God's actions in their lives. The joy of this encounter is difficult to hide or suppress! I wonder what it would be like if we tried a bit of *lectio* during a weekday Mass. If we usually preach three to five minutes, why not do a brief version of *lectio* with the people? What word struck you? Share it with someone sitting near you. Again, what struck you? Why do you think that word stood out for you? Less than five minutes. People would begin to love it, and their enthusiasm would energize them to lead small prayer groups themselves!

Work hard to be sure the sacraments, especially Eucharist and reconciliation, are available and attractive for people. Yes, "if you build it, they will come!" The arts—visual, musical—all attract people to God who is beauty.

What more can we say about being a welcoming community? If the people themselves *care* enough to be welcoming, newcomers, visitors, and even old-timers will notice. Hospitality is contagious! The issue of parish activities is often difficult since some parishioners feel proprietary about certain groups and activities. With patience and good humor, this needs to be addressed, for the sake of evangelization.

Then we look beyond our walls to the other faith communities in the area. Socialize together first, then pray together. A few experiences of *sharing* with one another go a long way to dispel stereotypes and myths that keep us apart. A parish near our motherhouse hosts a Ramadan meal each year. The Muslim community presides and provides the foods, but the Catholic Church hall is large enough and the Muslim and Christian people are thrilled to be invited.

Perhaps one of the most powerful tools of evangelizing our own people is a lively adult education. They need to know their faith if they *dare* to share it effectively. Education helps banish the demons of helplessness, incorrect beliefs, and myths that hinder their confidence. Make the program attractive, using varied media, games, contests, and handouts for all. Some have found family catechesis to be effective, and it affects the parish as well. RCIA is a place where many cradle Catholics discover their faith as they assist with initiating new members. Service projects are innumerable in Catholic communities, but do we ever call them evangelization? Why not? It is where we see God at work right in front of our eyes. It gives people a chance to speak of why they do what they do, too.

Whether people are old or young, able or challenged, there are ways for every one of us to evangelize, to proclaim God's good news. As Archbishop Oscar Romero famously remarked, "Everyone can do something!" There is no greater guarantee than the words of Jesus, "I am with you always," as we walk the winding, often uphill road of evangelization. Expect blessings!

Endnotes

1. Paul VI, *Evangelii Nuntiandi* 14.

2. Devon Wolfe, "Planting Seeds of Faith," *The Word Among Us* (February 2014): 61.

3. Andrew Dubois, "The New Evangelization: Hospitality is at the Heart," *Harvest: The Magazine of the Catholic Diocese of Portland* 7, no. 5 (September/October 2012): 2; http://faithdigital.org/harvest/PO0912/#?page=2.

4. Peter Vaghi, "Encountering Jesus," *America* 210, no. 9 (March 17, 2014): 23.

5. See Pope Francis, *Evangelii Gaudium* 78.

6. Bruno Cadoré, OP, Letter to the Brothers and Sisters of the Order of Preachers, December 22, 2013.

Chapter 4

Preaching with Evangelical Dynamism

Jude Siciliano, OP

I find it ironic that I have become a giver of preaching workshops. I have been a preacher since my ordination forty-five years ago in the Dominican Order. When I graduated from college and pursued my vocational instincts, I went to the Paulist Fathers in Manhattan and was told that the charism of the Paulists is "to preach to Main Street America." Since I wanted to be a college literature teacher and a priest, I wanted nothing to do with preaching, so I joined the Order of Preachers. The irony! Or, God's sense of humor.

Since my focus is "dynamic preaching," and since most of us are preachers and ministers involved in liturgical practice, I have chosen the gospel for the feast of Saints Peter and Paul for our focus. Since I am a working preacher, I would find it helpful to get input for this Sunday's homily. Let's start by listening to the poem "Leisure," by W. H. Davies:

> What is this life if, full of care,
> We have no time to stand and stare?—
> No time to stand beneath the boughs,
> And stare as long as sheep and cows:
> No time to see, when woods we pass,
> Where squirrels hide their nuts in grass:
> No time to see, in broad daylight,
> Streams full of stars, like skies at night:

> No time to turn at Beauty's glance,
> And watch her feet, how they can dance:
> No time to wait till her mouth can
> Enrich that smile her eyes began?
> A poor life this if, full of care,
> We have no time to stand and stare.[1]

Despite the poem's title, it speaks to the "work" of preaching. I'm going to suggest that the way we listen to poetry is the way we also should listen to the Scriptures—letting the words soak in, dwelling in images, and attending to what we see and hear in our reflection.

Pope Francis seems to suggest the same type of receptivity to the Scriptures. His apostolic exhortation *Evangelii Gaudium* has been a thrill for us Dominicans because he seemed to be writing to us. He wrote on preaching and evangelization! One of his key points is that we need to practice the art of listening. We just spent a short period of time listening to this poem. The poem addresses us preachers, who have the responsibility, the pope tells us, of serious preparation. Yet, because we are so busy, our temptation is to rush ahead to get the task done. How could that rush ever produce "dynamic preaching"?

Both the poem and Pope Francis suggest that we "stop and stare." Speaking to preachers, the pope gives helpful hints for beginning the preaching preparation stage. He instructs us to begin by listening. He even suggests how we might do this: "There is one particular way of listening to what the Lord wishes to tell us in his word and of letting ourselves be transformed by the Spirit. It is what we call *lectio divina*. It consists of reading God's word in a moment of prayer and allowing it to enlighten and renew us. This prayerful reading of the Bible is not something separate. . . . " (*Evangelii Gaudium* 152). Or, as the poet might advise: as we approach the Scriptures we must first "stop and stare." The pope says that we preachers must be the first to let the word of God move us deeply. "We need to let ourselves be penetrated by that word which will also penetrate others" (ibid. 150).

Pope Francis says that after being nourished by the Word the preacher must witness to it. The pope's reference to witnessing to the word of God hearkens back to Pope Paul VI's 1975 encyclical, *Evangelii Nuntiandi*, in which he says, "Modern [persons] listen more willingly to witnesses than to teachers, and if [they] listen to teachers, it is because they are witnesses" (41). We know that the word "witness" in the Bible means martyr. I can attest to a certain kind of "martyrdom" in my experience as a preacher. For the first thirty or so years of preaching I was *extremely* nervous each time I preached. (Now I'm *just* nervous!) I felt like I was shedding blood preparing and then preaching. There is a dying to self in this preaching process as we struggle to be open to the Word. We Dominicans have a saying that speaks to a certain kind of martyrdom: "The wood of our desk is the wood of our cross." One of the places dying happens for the preacher is at the desk.

The title of this piece is "Preaching with Evangelical Dynamism." The Oxford English Dictionary defines the word "dynamic" as "characterized by constant change, activity, or progress." Note, these are *action* words. The dictionary also says "dynamic" is related to "dynamite." So how to get evangelical dynamism in our preaching? Pope Francis suggests we start with silence. We begin the preparation process by following the pope's advice: we first keep a silence with the Word. We must invest more time in silence if we are to hear anything that will nourish us and our listeners. In the silence we are listening to self, people, the Scriptures, the environment, the world. So, let's call the first step of preparation a "listening step." We go to the Scriptures remembering that the word of God is active—it does what it says. And so first we allow it to do what it says within us. Then having experienced the living and transformative power of the Word, we witness to it through our preaching.

So the first stage of preaching preparation is an intensive listening stage. What we don't want to do is leave this stage too soon. We will be tempted to "get on with it." We are relying on God's word to speak to us and we are in a period of waiting with anticipation. The pope has asked us preachers to do something I would be too timid to suggest because, when I preach in parishes, I can see how busy priests, deacons, and staff are. He says, "I presume to ask that each week a sufficient portion of personal and community time be dedicated to this task, even if less time has to be given to other important activities. Trust in the Holy Spirit, who is at work during the homily, is not merely passive but active and creative. It demands that we offer ourselves and all our abilities as instruments (cf. Rom 12:1) which God can use. A preacher who does not prepare is not 'spiritual'; he is dishonest and irresponsible with the gifts he has received" (*Evangelii Gaudium* 145).

Fred Craddock, a Protestant biblical scholar and homiletician, has a theology and spirituality of preaching based on God's word: "The way God's Word is in the world is the way of the sermon in the world. The

Word proceeds from silence."[2] Craddock says there is the silence of God; God does not talk all the time. So, for example, when the rabbis give a commentary on the first words of Genesis ("In the beginning . . . then God said, 'Let there be light,' and there was light") the rabbis ask, "What was God doing before God said, 'Let there be light'?" Their response, "Keeping silence." God was keeping a silence, and then God broke the silence. That is Craddock's definition of preaching: "The preacher breaks the silence." Of course, that presumes we first kept the silence. Instead of emphasizing gestures and vocal variations when we speak about "dynamic preaching," we begin by talking about silence.

The book of Wisdom (18:14-15) says that silence surrounds the coming of the word of God: "For when peaceful stillness [silence] encompassed everything / and the night in its swift course was half spent, / Your all-powerful word from heaven's royal throne / leaped into the doomed land." The Word is hardly a sluggard; it leaped from heaven.

It's not only about Jesus Christ taking flesh but also about preaching. God broke the silence with a creative word and said, "Let there be light. And there was light." Craddock says people sit waiting and asking, "Is there a word from the Lord?" There is, and preaching breaks the silence to bring it to a waiting community. That is why the preacher needs to design a pattern of preparation that begins with silence and listening— and then breaks the silence. Or, as we Dominicans would say, *Contemplata aliis tradere*. "We give to others the fruits of our contemplation." This presumes contemplative activities were part of the preparation process.

One way of listening, or contemplating, is to take the passage with us to various ministerial settings and read and pray it in those settings: at the bed of a sick person, with a prisoner, at a wake, in a Scripture class, with a person in spiritual direction, and so forth. What do we hear in those settings? What different and surprising word of grace emerges? We are listening for a word of grace. Not a "central theme"—forget themes! We don't preach themes.

After the first stage of preaching preparation, the intensive listening stage, we don't want to rush ahead to the next—a study stage that would have us turning to reference books, biblical commentaries, homilies written by others, and so on. We are relying on God's word to speak to us and we are trusting this process that begins with intentional and planned listening. As the poet suggested, we "stand and stare." The purpose or goal of this first stage is to arrive at the nutshell of the preaching. This is where the preaching is born. What are we listening for in this first stage of preparation?

Mary Catherine Hilkert, OP, in her book on the theology of preaching, says the task of the preacher is to "name the grace."[3] In other words, we discern and proclaim the active presence of God in our midst. The particular Scripture passage we are focusing on in our preparation will help us recognize and experience that presence. Then our preaching task is to help our hearers experience God actively present in their lives.

How would we summarize what we have been listening for and striving to preach? We can summarize the fruits of our listening in two brief statements. First, we ask, What is God doing in this passage? (Note the emphasis on action.) Second, As a result of what God is doing, how are we able to respond? These summary statements are a way of summing up the presence and activity of grace in our lives.

When I studied preaching we were told to develop and preach a "central idea" that could summarize in one sentence the message of the preaching. But by doing that the preaching tends to focus on ideas and lacks movement. Preaching is not primarily about conveying ideas—it's about naming God's active presence in our world and showing how we are enabled to respond to that presence.

When we arrive at the two summary statements we have come to the end of "stage one" of our preparation.

Here is how the American bishops described the liturgical homily in their document *Fulfilled in Your Hearing*: "a scriptural interpretation of human existence which enables a community to recognize God's active presence, to respond to that presence in faith through liturgical word and gesture, and beyond the liturgical assembly, through a life lived in conformity with the Gospel."[4] Notice that the community is *enabled* by the recognition of God's active presence in its midst. In the South, where I have spent most of my ministry, some preachers would put it this way: "The indicative precedes the imperative." First, we hear the statement of the Good News (the indicative); then, we are able to respond to its call to conversion and service to our sisters and brothers (the imperative).

I remember the advice given to me by a senior preacher: "Keep it simple, stupid!" I think Mary Oliver said a similar thing in her poem "Praying." She suggests to preachers what we must do:

> It doesn't have to be
> the blue iris, it could be
> weeds in a vacant lot, or a few
> small stones; just
> pay attention, then patch

> a few words together and don't try
> to make them elaborate, this isn't
> a contest but the doorway
>
> into thanks, and a silence in which
> another voice may speak.[5]

Oliver's image of a "doorway into thanks" suggests a sequence for us. The preaching should move us to the next stage in the liturgical celebration. If we are preaching at a Eucharist, the homily is our entrance into the eucharistic celebration that follows the preaching and it gives us words and stirs up feelings with which to express "thanks."

Since I listen to a lot of preaching in my travels to parishes around the country, I would like to name some things I think can short-circuit "dynamic preaching." These are a few of the heresies and bad practices I hear in preaching.

1. *The preacher engages in moralizing and Pelagianism.* In these preachings one hears encouragement to work hard to follow the moral teachings of the gospel. It seems the preacher reads the passage to look for what the Bible tells us we must *do*. Then, the preacher suggests, if we do it God will reward us. Along with this, Jesus is proposed as a "model" for right behavior. If we follow his example, we will earn our reward from God. Of course, there is no Savior or Good News in that, is there?

2. *There is a lack of focus.* The preacher jumps from one reading to another. We don't always have to preach from the gospel; we can choose another reading that has spoken to us. But if we do, stay with that reading and proclaim the God of grace in it. Yes, even from the Hebrew text!

3. *The preacher speaks about the text, preaching* on *the text but not* from *it.* It is a preaching about the text. We can avoid this didactic tendency if we draw from the fruits of the first, listening stage of our preparation.

4. *The preacher sounds detached from the reading.* He seems to interpret his task as explaining the reading to us. The preacher is not "in the reading," but out of the mix. It is like a doctor coming to the side of a sick person prescribing what he or she must do to get better. Remember, the pope said we need witnesses, not teachers.

5. *Lectors are not well trained.* Lectors need to be instructed on how to proclaim the story of the Bible in a way that grabs and holds the attention of the listeners.

6. *There is too much focus on missalettes.* Forget the missalettes, except for the hard of hearing. Without them we are listening together, being formed

into a community together. With missalettes people have their heads buried in them and, because we read at different speeds, the effect is a scattered and detached community, each at a different place in the passage.

7. *Preachers do not ask for feedback.* If we do not ask for feedback, how would we know what people are hearing or how we look while we are preaching?

Endnotes

1. W. H. Davies, "Leisure," in *Songs of Joy and Others* (London: A. C. Fifield, 1911).

2. Fred Craddock, *Preaching* (Nashville: Abingdon Press, 1985), 53.

3. Mary Catherine Hilkert, *Naming Grace: Preaching and the Sacramental Imagination* (New York: Continuum, 1997).

4. USCCB, *Fulfilled in Your Hearing: The Homily in the Sunday Assembly* (Washington, DC: USCCB, 1982), 29.

5. Mary Oliver, "Praying," in *Thirst* (Boston: Beacon Press, 2006).

Chapter 5

Preaching and the Rites of Initiation

Paul Turner

I have a confession to make. In my parish, when I preside for various rites of initiation, I sometimes choose not to preach about them. I preach from the Scriptures on some other theme that I feel the community may need to hear instead. Here is why: I treat the homily as a literary unit, like an essay. I think it should develop one thought. I don't think it needs to embrace all the circumstances of the day—a survey of all the readings including the psalm, a nod to the day's feast or season, an expression of appreciation for groups in attendance, or a further explanation of a rite celebrated at that Mass. The homily is not an after-dinner speech. The rites themselves are descriptive, and they may not need further cate-chesis. Besides, the liturgy provides other moments when the presider or someone else may insert comments. For example, after the greeting, an introduction to the ceremonies of the day may be given. The prayer of the faithful may include petitions for specific groups. Before the eu-charistic prayer, reasons for thanksgiving may be noted. If there is a natural fit within the homily I'm developing, I will make it. But I some-times feel that preaching about an initiation rite is forced. Often I don't do it. I trust the rite to convey its own meaning.

However, there are many rites of initiation in the Catholic Church, and some of them do warrant a special homily. I will survey the principal rites for the initiation of adults and children, making remarks about what may or may not be helpful in preaching for them.

All of these rites presume some form of evangelization. Here I'm speaking of evangelization in its first sense: bringing the Gospel to those who have not yet heard it or engaged with it. I am not speaking of its derivative sense, in which we all need to meet the Gospel again and again, and are thereby evangelized by its message. The initiation rites of the Catholic Church presume that someone among the faithful has invited a friend or a spouse to meet Jesus Christ and hear his word. They presume that parents sincerely desire to hand their faith on to their children. The rites monitor the evangelization that is under way, and the homily—whatever its theme—becomes part of this very evangelization.

Let's begin, then, with the Rite of Christian Initiation of Adults. Its first rite is called Acceptance into the Order of Catechumens. It is the ceremony whereby those who have not been baptized publicly proclaim their first acceptance of the Gospel, and the church asserts its willingness to provide support and formation. The rite may be celebrated at a Sunday Mass; however the liturgical books envision that it takes place at a Liturgy of the Word, probably because in some parts of the world, the unbaptized are so unfamiliar with Mass that having them participate with the Sunday assembly in any way may seem disorienting. I generally do celebrate this rite at Sunday Mass, and when I ask those aspiring to be catechumens to tell the parish community what they are asking for and why, you can hear a pin drop as they speak their fledgling faith out loud to us for the first time.

At Sunday Mass, a homily about this ceremony may be superfluous because the rite itself is so expressive. However, a good homily can be preached about its themes of faith, as would definitely be done if celebrated outside of Mass. The principal theme of this ceremony is the foundations of faith—a first awareness of God, who sent Jesus into the world to make us disciples. The Rite of Acceptance establishes a canonical relationship between the catechumen and the rest of the community. The catechumen will enjoy certain rights, such as marriage in the church or, God forbid, a Christian funeral. However, the ceremony is not about Catholicism; it's about evangelization. It is not the time to preach about how Catholics differ from other Christians, but how we Christians differ from everyone else. "RCIA" is not the "Rite of Catholic Initiation of Adults." It's the Rite of Christian Initiation of Adults. It brings the unbaptized to baptism. The Rite of Acceptance directly links to evangelization. It uses primary symbols of our faith: signing people with the cross, inviting them to pass over the threshold of the church, giving them a place in the community, and stressing the importance of the Bible as the guide of our formation. A homily about this occasion should stress discipleship to Jesus Christ.

During the period of the catechumenate, those undergoing formation may receive an anointing with the oil of catechumens, as well as special prayers of exorcism and blessing. These rites are not often celebrated on Sundays, but they may be. For example, after the homily, catechumens may come forward for an anointing, and this may be done more than once. The homily on such an occasion could handle themes of the struggles in the spiritual life and the help that the church affords through sign and symbol. The oil of catechumens is a kind of protective oil. It keeps evil forces away. It works like a spiritual mosquito repellent or sunscreen, protecting the catechumen from harm. A homily already developing such a theme might incorporate a reference to the oil of catechumens, but otherwise the prayers of the liturgy should provide sufficient catechetical content.

The period of the catechumenate closes with the Rite of Election or Enrollment of Names. Customarily this is celebrated as a diocesan event with the bishop presiding at the cathedral. In the United States, most but not all dioceses combine the Rite of Election with the Call to Continuing Conversion for baptized candidates who will be received into the full communion of the Catholic Church at the Easter Vigil. The preaching is absolutely central. There is no other theme the bishop should explore but the meaning of the ceremony. However, a homilist often pursues the wrong trail for two reasons: the choice of readings and the presence of the baptized candidates.

With regard to the readings, the Rite of Election is frequently celebrated on the Saturday following Ash Wednesday, or on the afternoon of the First Sunday of Lent. Almost everyone celebrates it as a Liturgy of the Word because the primary participants are not yet eligible for Communion. However, the RCIA thinks that the Rite of Election is taking place on the First Sunday of Lent at the community's Mass. Planners often move it to a weekday, or at least to a time on Sunday when no one is gathering for the Eucharist, so that it won't conflict. The discrepancy has caused those preparing the celebration to abandon the readings assigned to the Rite of Election and compile their own. These sometimes adopt themes from Lent or even Easter as a way of exploring election.

However, the readings are supposed to be those for Mass on the First Sunday of Lent. The gospel should be the temptation in the desert, which sets the stage for the spiritual battle between right and wrong that the elect will engage during the upcoming scrutinies and throughout their period of purification and enlightenment that extends from this ceremony up until their initiation at Easter.

With baptized candidates present, the Rite of Election has become a hybrid of election and Lenten preparation. The word "election" calls to mind the chosen people of the Old Testament. Just as God chose a people for a covenant of old, so we believe that God is choosing a people today for entrance into a new covenant with Jesus Christ. As the first chosen people crossed the waters of the Red Sea into freedom, and the waters of the Jordan into their own Promised Land, so the new chosen people pass through the waters of baptism to claim freedom in Christ and their hopes for heaven. This is neatly captured in the climax of the Rite of Election, when the bishop says, "I now declare you to be members of the elect, to be initiated into the sacred mysteries at the next Easter Vigil" (RCIA 133). The Call to Continuing Conversion, however, has no comparable richness. The baptized candidates are already elect. They already stand on the same shores of baptism as the Catholics who are present. So, the bishop delivers a separate message to them at the climax of their ceremony: "the Church recognizes your desire (to be sealed with the gift of the Holy Spirit and) to have a place at Christ's eucharistic table. Join with us this Lent in a spirit of repentance. Hear the Lord's call to conversion and be faithful to your baptismal covenant" (RCIA 454). In so many words, the bishop is making this pronouncement: "Have a nice Lent." The occasion tempts the homilist to stress what the Catholic Church offers that other churches do not: a pope, the Eucharist, seven sacraments, devotion to Mary, and so forth. The theme of the Rite of Election is not the Catholic Church, but divine election—the choice of God who invites specific people to the waters of baptism and life in Christ. The Rite of Election extends a further arm of evangelization, drawing those who were unfamiliar with the Gospel closer to a covenant with Jesus Christ.

One of the more controversial rites for preachers is the scrutinies. "Scrutiny" is a word for which we need another word. It's not the most welcoming expression in the lexicon of evangelization. "Come on over! Ask us about the Catholic Church, and we'll give you a scrutiny!" But it is the word that comes down to us through the history of the catechumenate, and it has its origins in the opening verses of Psalm 139: "O LORD, you search me [or "scrutinize" me] and you know me. / You yourself know my resting and my rising; / you discern my thoughts from afar. / You mark when I walk or lie down; / you know all my ways through and through" (Revised Grail Psalter). During the scrutinies the church prays that the elect will approach initiation with proper motives and a pure heart. To that end, scrutinies include exorcisms, during which the priest imposes hands upon the elect. These are not your Hollywood-head-spinning-split-pea-soup-spewing kind of exorcisms, but ones that rescue the unbaptized human from the lure of sin. Those who are baptized have a sacramental advantage over the unbaptized. Children of God in Christ, they have spiritual aids to tame evil. The unbaptized do not yet share this advantage; hence their susceptibility to sin, sacramentally speaking, is wild. The exorcisms in the scrutinies drive away whatever keeps the elect from committing themselves to Christ while strengthening the positive growth already begun.

The scrutinies are supposed to take place on Sundays, and they are so important that to do fewer than three requires the permission of the bishop (RCIA 34/3). Very few priests know that they are supposed to solicit this permission, and even fewer bishops know that they give it. Nonetheless, this provision shows how seriously the church takes the scrutiny rites.

For preachers, the scrutinies pose a unique problem. The prayers for the exorcisms link to the gospel passages that are proclaimed from the Lectionary for Mass in Year A for Sundays 3, 4, and 5 of Lent: the woman at the well, the man born blind, and the raising of Lazarus—all from John's gospel. During Years B and C of the cycle, if you have scrutinies at Mass on those Sundays, the assembly is supposed to hear the Year A gospels. In fact, if for some serious reason you plan to baptize an adult at some other time of year, the sacrament should be preceded by a non-Lenten period of purification and enlightenment; the scrutinies should take place on three Sundays, even if it is Ordinary Time, and the scrutiny gospels replace *those* readings. More commonly the situation arises during Lectionary years B and C during Lent. It challenges preachers, as well as musicians, who usually prepare for multiple weekend Masses with one set of Scriptures in mind. If you have more than one preacher in the parish, one could prepare the scrutiny homily while the others handle the remaining Masses. In many parishes, though, this is not an option. In those cases, preachers are essentially being told: prepare two homilies. Some of them choose a different solution: they simply refuse to use the readings from Year A. As a result, huffy members of the cate-chumenate team complain about uncooperative priests, who in turn argue that they are just trying to manage an already crowded weekend of parish life. However, there has been a slight change in the legislation between the publication of the 1972 typical edition of the RCIA and the 2008 third edition of the Roman Missal. The 1972 edition said that the readings of Year A were to be used at scrutiny Masses in Years B and C. The 2008 third edition of the Missal, translated into English in 2011, has a slightly different legislation. It doesn't say that the Year A readings are proclaimed, but the Year A gospels are. This should be good news for preachers. They can prepare a homily about the first reading, the psalm, or the second reading, or about the penitential rite or the Lamb of God or some phrase from the Creed, and use the same homily all weekend, including the scrutiny Mass. Perhaps the homily will address the themes of the scrutiny, perhaps not. But if it does, it should help people under-stand the power of Christ over Satan, the ultimate impotence of sin and death, and the hope we have amid the trials of life. These are valuable themes for all in the Christian life, though especially for those approach-ing the waters of baptism.

The post–Vatican II Lent has a double focus. It has always provided spiritual renewal for the faithful who on Ash Wednesday receive the mark of sinfulness and the threat of death. This focus continues, but Lent also provides spiritual preparation for the elect. The Year C gospels for Sundays 3, 4, and 5 especially focus on the renewal of those already baptized: the barren fig tree, the parable of the Prodigal Son, and the story of the woman caught in adultery. All these offer hope to the sin-ner who repents. Year B's gospels anticipate the events of Holy Week: Jesus driving the money changers from the temple, Jesus telling Nico-demus that the Son of Man must be lifted up like the serpent in the desert, and Jesus informing Andrew and Philip that the grain of wheat must fall to the earth and die. Only the Year A gospels clearly focus on the path to baptism.

Lent includes two other rites for the elect, the presentation of the Creed and of the Lord's Prayer. These too have a long history in the liturgy of the church. They are occasions on which the community hands on to the elect two of its greatest treasures. The presentation rites are not supposed to take place on Sundays. I generally choose a weeknight when something else is going on, for example, Stations of the Cross, a meeting of the Knights of Columbus, or a Lenten Mass. The presentations can be anticipated even months before the Rite of Election if the parish has too many activities during Lent. But the long tradition is that they form part of the immediate preparation for baptism. For example, some of the church fathers used the Creed as the springboard for pre-baptismal cate-chesis. It became the spiritual textbook that helped the elect prepare to make their baptismal promises, just as the scrutinies prepared the elect to renounce sin. The presentation of the Creed traditionally follows the first scrutiny; the elect don't receive the Creed until purification is under way. You don't get a blood transfusion until your arm has been cleansed.

The presentation of the Lord's Prayer was always made near the end of Lent. Saint Augustine did it on Holy Saturday. That is still an option, though more commonly it takes place on a weekday after the Fifth Sun-day of Lent. The Lord's Prayer is strong food, so the elect receive it near the end of their preparation. After surgery a patient may advance through a liquid diet before taking food to chew. Even though many unbaptized believers say the Lord's Prayer daily, the opening words will have more meaning after baptism. Jesus Christ is the only begotten Son of God, and we the baptized are children of God by adoption. That entitles us with Christ to call God our Father.

The presentations of the Creed and the Lord's Prayer take place at small gatherings during Lent. They include a Liturgy of the Word and homily, not the Eucharist. Because of the nature of the event, no conflict-ing purposes are present, and the homily should address the rite. For the presentation of the Creed, the homilist may treat the importance of this system of belief for the community. After a good homily, the people will recite the Creed with great intensity, to pass the words of their faith to a new generation of believers.

The presentation of the Lord's Prayer occurs in the proclamation of the gospel, done by the priest, even if a deacon is assisting. The priest is the presider of the entire ceremony, so he presents the Lord's Prayer. He gathers the elect directly in front of the ambo and proclaims the pertinent passage from Matthew 6. As Jesus taught the prayer to his disciples, so his voice, through the proclaimed gospel, reaches the ears of the elect. The preacher should address the ceremony at hand, speaking about the prayer that Jesus taught us, and especially its opening words. English is one of the few languages that requires an adjectival personal pronoun to precede the noun it modifies. In the original Greek, in Latin, in Span-ish, in German, and in many other languages, the very first word of the prayer is "Father." The second word is "our." "Father" should be the focus of the preaching on this occasion, not just who God is under this title, but who we are, who are entitled to use this title whenever we address God.

The Mass of chrism is not properly a rite of initiation, but it is relevant to the initiation rites. The reason chrism is consecrated near the end of Lent is to provide a fresh supply for the rites of initiation at the Easter Vigil. For the sake of convenience, while the bishop is consecrating chrism, he blesses the other oils used in the administration of the sacraments, the oil of catechumens and the oil of the sick. Two of these oils, then, especially pertain to the catechumenate. One would think that the homily at the Mass of chrism would make this point. Normally, it does not. In the postconciliar revisions of the chrism Mass, a renewal of priests' promises was affixed to it with all the delicacy of duct tape. At the time, the Mass of chrism was always celebrated on Holy Thursday, broadly interpreted as the day when Jesus instituted the sacrament of holy orders at the Last Supper. In the 1960s when many priests were rethinking their commitment to the ministry, Holy Thursday morning, when priests concelebrated with the bishop, seemed like a good logistical choice for renewing promises.

Now, however, the Mass of chrism may be celebrated earlier than Holy Thursday, and that separation breaks the link between this Mass and the Last Supper. However, the renewal of promises remains. With the number of priests concelebrating and renewing their promises, the chrism Mass has turned into a festival for priests. The homily often reflects this interpretation. The readings and prayers of the day, however, give other testimony. All the readings apply to the anointing of the baptized. From Revelation we hear how Christ made us all a kingdom of priests. Isaiah says that God has anointed him to announce good news, and Jesus in the gospel proclaims that he fulfills Isaiah's prophecy. The psalm recalls the anointing of David. Jesus is the anointed one of God, and all the baptized share in this mystery. The collect for the chrism Mass also sounds the theme of the universal priesthood of the baptized: "O God, who anointed your Only Begotten Son with the Holy Spirit / and made him Christ and Lord, / graciously grant / that, being made sharers in his consecration, / we may bear witness to your Redemption in the world. / Through our Lord Jesus Christ, your Son . . . " That prayer stresses the gathering of those who have been consecrated, that is, anointed, in baptism. Even the prayer for the consecration of chrism has nothing to do with the ministerial priesthood, everything to do with baptism. Hence, although the chrism Mass is not one of the rites of initiation, it runs parallel to them and supports them. Yet the homily of the day often treats a subsidiary theme. Far better would be for all those gathered, laity and clergy alike, to hear about the significance of the oils in the sacramental life of those who follow Christ.

On the day before Easter, those to be baptized may participate in the Preparation Rites. These ceremonies may include the *Ephphetha*, the recitation of the Creed, and even the presentation of the Lord's Prayer. If the Lord's Prayer has already been presented, then the logical gospel passage for this event is the miraculous cure of the deaf man with a speech impediment. On that occasion, the Aramaic word Jesus uttered must have rung so powerfully not just in the ears of the infirm but in those of the bystanders as well that it was retained in Matthew's otherwise original Greek. Certain elements of this story make it especially beloved in the history of the catechumenate. The man is brought to Jesus by his friends, who act in a way similar to evangelizers and sponsors today; they ask for hand-laying, similar to the gesture incorporated in exorcisms; Jesus takes the man apart from the crowd, as catechumens were dismissed from the liturgy for their formation; Jesus works the miracle through words and actions, as is practiced in the Christian sacraments. Even though the *Ephphetha* rite has appeared among pre-baptismal ceremonies for many centuries, only after the Second Vatican Council has it included the proclamation of the originating passage, Matthew 7:31-37. A simple homily may prepare for the coming initiation rites. As the elect have opened their ears to the gospel, now we pray that their mouths may proclaim the wonders they are about to experience.

That brings us to the sacraments of initiation themselves, celebrated during the Easter Vigil. The resurrection of Christ blends seamlessly with baptism. The homily will precede the baptisms, but it can still speak about their significance. Baptism is one of the symbols of the resurrection. Some people wonder, When during the Easter Vigil do we celebrate the actual moment of Jesus rising from the dead? Is it at the fire? the *Exsultet*? the Gloria? the Alleluia? Well, it's all of these. The Vigil unfolds the mystery of the resurrection in layers. Before Vatican II the liturgy had two distinct parts, a Vigil and a Mass. Easter did not begin until the Gloria, when the altar candles were lighted. Today, the altar candles are still lighted during the Gloria, but the whole Vigil is considered one celebration of the Eucharist. It presents manifold images of the risen Christ: the lighting of the paschal candle and its procession into the church like the pillar of fire leading Israel from slavery to freedom; the singing of the Gloria to highlight the solemnity and joy of the day; the chanting of the Alleluia for the first time since before Ash Wednesday; the proclamation of the gospel of the resurrection, through which the risen Christ speaks to the gathered community; the baptisms, in which those who have been preparing for membership in the Body of Christ become children of God by adoption; and the Eucharist, when the entire community shares the sacramental Body and Blood of the risen Christ for the first time on Easter Day. A homily could explore any of these themes, linking the initiation rites to our belief in the resurrection, and guiding us under sacramental signs to the hope of future glory.

The Easter Vigil is still not very well attended in the average parish community, but it is the single most important celebration of the Eucharist each year, and the homily should reflect it. It requires extra care and attention. On days such as Easter and Christmas, originating events such as weddings and funerals, I think the homily needs to stay "close to the bone." The central theme of the homily should adhere to the celebration under way. If it's Christmas, the main theme should be something like "Christ is born for us." You can package that in a hundred different ways, but when people go home from that celebration, they should remember the significance of the incarnation and the difference it makes in their lives. For Easter, the basic theme of the homily I think should be "Christ is risen." Once again, you can make the point in a hundred different ways, with stories and images, biblical and liturgical references. But the tone of the homily should redound with joy, and its message should lift the hearts of all believers. The resurrection we celebrate is not merely a historical event, but one in which we may participate. Easter is different from Christmas. We will never participate in the incarnation the way Jesus did, but we may share his resurrection. That good news needs to be proclaimed, especially at the Easter Vigil.

For the next fifty days the newly baptized are invited to church with their godparents, taking seats with the rest of the assembly. This is the period of mystagogy, and its centerpiece is the Sunday homily. RCIA 245 says that the neophytes are "introduced into a fuller and more effective understanding of mysteries through the Gospel message they have learned and above all through their experience of the sacraments they have received." They are to take part in the neophyte Masses of the Sundays of Easter. The readings from Year A are especially highlighted; they include excerpts from the First Letter of Peter, which carries so many baptismal themes that some wonder if it is an early example of preaching on initiation. Hence, the preaching during the Easter season is supposed to be mystagogy. What does that mean?

Fine studies have been made by authors such as William Harmless, Craig Satterlee, and Lester Ruth. In general, they speak about the way preachers adopt a certain playfulness with symbols. They can start with any of the signs from the initiation rites: water, oil, bread, wine, processions, fire, readings, or prayers. Then they expand on the role of these symbols in ordinary life. Water gives life, but it also destroys; oil protects, but its aroma also pleases; bread is broken, and it is shared; wine comes from crushed grapes, yet it causes inebriating joy. Any of these symbols can help people connect everyday life with the extraordinary opportunity of life in Christ.

However, there are several challenges with mystagogical preaching in the Roman Rite today. In the early church, mystagogy took place during the first week of Easter. The newly baptized gathered at the cathedral with the bishop and heard, in some cases, extraordinary preaching about the sacraments they had received. These had not been fully explained to them beforehand, having been part of the *disciplina arcani*, or hidden formation, so the neophytes were hearing for the first time an explanation about these rites that they had so wondrously experienced days earlier. The memory of the events was fresh, and interest had peaked. In the post–Vatican II restored catechumenate, the framers of the rite probably thought it was impractical for the newly baptized to return to church every day for a week, and for priests or bishops to preach at length about the ceremonies every day, having just exhausted themselves with the Triduum. So they stretched out the mystagogical days to a week of weeks, seven Sundays, not seven weekdays. The presidential prayers at Mass during the Easter octave come from an ancient tradition and still presume that the neophytes have come for the Eucharist, but the RCIA never mentions it. This gives us a seven-week mystagogical timetable that never before existed. It is hard on the third, fourth, fifth, seventh Sunday after the Easter Vigil to recall the events of initiation; everybody has moved on. Besides, these Sundays fall during the year's busiest month, May, when Mother's Day, anniversaries, and graduations vie for attention on the calendar. It is impractical to preach only about the initiation rites for seven weeks when so many other demands crowd the table. Still, it can be done if the preacher chooses to think back to the Easter Vigil for inspiration to drive the homily's argument.

The RCIA proposes other occasions for the newly baptized to assemble. For example, it suggests celebrating Eucharist with the bishop. In some ways this appeals more than having him preside at the Rite of Election. Ideally, if the bishop as the father of the diocese can only be present once in the entire process of initiation, he should baptize all the elect at Easter. Logistically, this is nearly impossible. So what is second best? The Rite of Election has won out, but it would be equally important, if not more so, for the bishop to celebrate Eucharist with the newly baptized. He could then offer some mystagogical preaching of his own.

Finally, the RCIA suggests that the neophytes celebrate the anniversary of their baptism. The Missal formerly included a set of presidential prayers for such an occasion, though they were dropped after the Second Vatican Council. Nonetheless, the RCIA still recommends a reunion. Does this mean they should gather at the next Easter Vigil? Or on the anniversary date of their baptism? It doesn't say, but the next Easter Vigil makes a good choice. The homily that blends themes of the resurrection of Christ with the sacraments of initiation will also warm the hearts of those remembering their baptism one year ago.

Apart from adult initiation, homilies also pertain to the initiation of infants and children. The baptism of infants may take place outside of Mass or during it. I always prefer to baptize during a Sunday Mass so that the entire community may witness the spiritual birth of new members and support growing families. Some parishes have too many baptisms for this approach, but where the number is manageable, baptizing can enliven Sunday Mass. I generally do not preach about the baptism, but continue my practice of preaching about the readings. If there is a natural fit to the baptism, I make some allusion, but I do not make it a priority in the homily. The rites of baptism during Mass unfold at the very beginning, after the homily, before the Lord's Prayer, and during the final blessing. There are plenty of words addressed to the parents, family, and community; there are even some words addressed to the infant. In my opinion, the homily at a Sunday Mass does not need to include more. However, when baptism takes place outside of Mass, then, certainly a brief homily about the sacrament pertains. I usually improvise these based on the Scripture proclaimed. Baptisms outside of Mass are normally poor expressions of liturgical celebration. In most parishes these take place on Sunday afternoons when the community has dispersed and other ministers have gone home. Baptisms outside of Mass usually have no music for everyone to sing, an abbreviated Liturgy of the Word, an impromptu homily, and an informality that keeps the occasion light and enjoyable but remote from the quality of worship that parishes can offer during a Sunday Mass. Ideally, a baptism outside of Mass would have it all: parish musicians who would select appropriate music and lead it several times during the ceremony, processions from door to word to font to altar, several people proclaiming the readings, a homily prepared to move hearts and inspire those who gather infrequently at church, and a general sense of prayer and participation. But that's not happening, and we're usually too tired after the Masses on Sunday to introduce this change. The homily is only one symptom of the challenge.

Confirmation is usually celebrated by a bishop, and he usually preaches about the sacrament, as he should. However, the theology of confirmation is poorly understood, and the homily can range across quite a number of topics, like a metal detector in an open field, searching for lost coins. Some bishops retain a former practice of turning the homily into a final exam, to see if the students really have learned their catechesis. For a homily close to the bone, the basic message should be that confirmation is a gift of the Holy Spirit and that the confirmed should now share that gift with the community.

I admit, though, that at confirmation this year with members of my own parish, most of whom speak only Spanish, I found myself wishing that the bishop would communicate pastoral messages to the parents: the importance of annual religious education for children, instead of single-year sacramental preparation for First Communion and confirmation; the beauty of sacramental marriage in the Catholic Church, which is sorely neglected in the Hispanic community; the joy of receiving Communion, which many Hispanics forsake for the joy of living with someone outside of marriage, a decision they justify by a corollary belief learned from priests and catechists: one should feel unworthy in the presence of the Blessed Sacrament and be content to adore, not to receive. I think our people need to hear these themes from the top, and I caught myself wishing that the bishop would use the occasion of a confirmation homily to deliver catechesis to parents. It's not a very liturgical way of preaching, but it would instill sacramental values that we badly need.

First Communion Masses are often celebrated apart from the Sunday liturgy, but they may take place during regular Sunday Masses; some parishes split the group so that families and parishioners can celebrate together on different occasions. The homily at a First Communion Mass may address the event or something more generic from the readings. A children's homily can be especially effective. A homily addressed to children will reach the adults, and it can incorporate techniques used at any Mass for students at a Catholic school, engaging the participation of the children through question and answer or even drama. The preacher should carefully think through the key idea to convey, and build the homily around it. If the idea is something like, "We want this to be your first Communion, not your last Communion," the parents will hear the message.

So, as you can see, the rites of initiation are many and complex, and preaching at them is just as complex. On some occasions the homily needs to be very explicit for the occasion being celebrated, but on others, especially when the rites are one part of the bigger celebration of a parish Sunday Mass, the homily could pursue another theme. The rites themselves convey sufficient meaning, and everyone could hear a homily more broadly based on themes for all those gathered on this day. Nonetheless, when preachers take the time to reflect upon the individuals preparing for initiation, the life stories that have brought them here, the Scriptures, prayers and ceremonies of the day, they will do the entire community a favor. They will reveal the power of the paschal mystery in the sacraments of the church, and they will draw the faithful to a realization of the demands and joys of faith.

Chapter 6

Made for Mission:
Evangelizing Young Adults

Curtis Martin

I'm excited about the topic of evangelizing young adults, but also I really believe that if we were to get this right, the principles apply to every other part of the generations. So we will be looking at the broader group, through the microscope of young adults.

What I would like to do is look at three areas of evangelizing young people and preaching. I want to confess right up front, I'm not a preacher so I will not teach you how to preach. I will share some principles with you that I think might apply to preaching, but focus instead on the way we use them as we are teaching Scripture in different venues and formats.

The first area is going to be out in the field, if you will, the non-preaching aspect of evangelization. Whether we are priests or laypeople or religious or what have you, we need to be out in the field. The second area is going to be within the liturgy, to look at the liturgy itself. The third area is going to look specifically at the use of Sacred Scripture, which is where I'll spend most of my time, but I think the other two areas are also very important.

Let me begin with a brief story, which I think will set the stage for our journey together. An elementary schoolteacher is teaching a class of students and she realizes that she is probably using some words the students don't actually know the definition of. She stops for a moment and says, "Does anyone in the room know the difference between ignorance and apathy?" She looks around and the students give her puzzled looks. "Can someone tell me the difference?" No one wants to speak up. Finally the teacher looks at the star student, Becky, and she asks her, "What is the difference between ignorance and apathy?" Becky thinks for a second then says, "I don't know and I don't care." This is precisely the difference between ignorance and apathy!

I think there has been a tremendous improvement in my lifetime in the Catholic Church, which I came back to in 1985. I don't know what your experience of the church in '85 was, but for me it was a bit confusing. I would read the fathers of the church and I would read the great saints, and I was like, yes, yes! But then I would look around and I couldn't find what I had read, in the church. There were different opinions and all these people under the banner of Catholicism with different teachings. Since then we have had the great body of work of Pope John Paul II. The *Catechism* came out and there's a lot more clarity. In fact, I don't know that there's ever been a better time in the history of the world in the English language to learn the Catholic faith. It's spectacular! We can learn the faith with clarity and certainty and it's a really wonderful time. And although that's great and I take nothing away from that, we need to get even better and more dedicated. The question of "Can you learn your faith?" addresses the issue of "I don't know," but that is not even the question of the day. The question of the day is "I don't care." That actually takes logical and chronological priority over "I don't know," because if you don't address the apathy issue, no amount of teaching is actually going to change lives. It would be a little bit like somebody coming to you hours after you finish one of the largest dinners of your life and saying, "Hey, surprise, you've been invited to a nine-course banquet just in the other room right now." And you would say, "That would be wonderful, but I'm stuffed! I have no hunger for food." Even if it is the best meal you could possibly serve me, because I have no appetite, I can't appreciate that gift.

I would argue that the truth and the beauties of the Catholic Church are coming alive like they haven't in many generations, such as the marriage of our love and truth, *Caritas in Veritate* (Pope Benedict XVI, 2009). This is an exciting time. The Catholic Church stands in the gap in the middle of the biggest issues of the day, shining light and truth and goodness into all these issues. It's an amazing time intellectually to be a Catholic. On the campuses where FOCUS (Fellowship of Catholic University Students) serves, such as Vanderbilt, Baylor, and Harvard, we are looking at high-level conversations taking place between people of faith and people who don't have faith, between Christians who are Protestant and Christians who are Catholic. Many in these conversations find themselves either desirous of becoming Catholic or at least jealous of Catholics, because it's a wonderful thing to have access to the fullness of truth. It doesn't mean that we always access the truth; we just have access. It's an amazing thing to look at two thousand years of tradition. But that is for people who actually have addressed the apathy issue already.

The apathy issue is the problem of the day. Many of our young people and people of all ages just don't care. It is not because they are uncaring people. We just live in the most highly distracted civilization in the history of the world. If you think about a farmer in the Middle Ages, he got up in the morning before the sun rose and would walk out into his field where he would strap himself into a plow and walk along back and forth, he and his ox, for hours and hours and hours. He would break for lunch then get back out and plow for hours and hours and hours. Finally he would get home and he would see his wife. She was the most beautiful thing that he had seen all day because all day he had been staring at the rear end of an ox, and by way of comparison, she was spectacular! That's not the case anymore. Today, men and women drive to work past airbrushed models with music blaring at them or televisions. Our young people today have no moment of silence in their life; everything is coming at them and they are radically distracted. In the Middle Ages, for young people the most exciting experience of their week was probably going to Mass. Mass was pageantry and music and smells and bells and storytelling. The rest of the week was pretty dull. The Mass hasn't changed substantially since that time, but it is now the most boring experience for young people in their entire week. We have been overwhelmed by a culture that has gotten much louder than we are. And the goal is not to raise our voice so that we can be even louder. It is to get better at telling our story. I believe, and I would like to share the theory with you, that the solution to this problem is relationship.

Our faith in a certain sense is all about relationship, because our life is all about relationships. We spend so much of our waking hours in this culture pursuing money so that we can get stuff so that we can be happy. But if you have all the money and all the stuff and no one to share it with, you still wouldn't be happy. However, if you have someone whom you love and you are loved by, even if you didn't have all the stuff and you didn't have all the money, you would experience authentic happiness.

When we send college students into developing countries, one of the most frequently stated comments by them is, "I couldn't believe these people who had nothing were so happy." It's because they have relationships. Catholicism is in reality, at its core, relationships. It is the revelation of the Blessed Trinity, three perfect persons, who live in eternal relationship, who extend that relationship, in the person of the Son, to us who are broken. Then we can be in a relationship. The Catechism tells us in original justice we experienced four harmonies: harmony with God, harmony within ourselves, harmony with other people, and harmony with creation. Original sin ruptured all four of those relationships. It is the work of the eternal Son, made man, to restore those relationships. And we, once we have encountered him, and are in relationship with him, become agents in restoring those relationships. Relationship is our home game. What do we do with it? I want to look at the areas I spoke about. First, out in the field; second, the liturgy itself in a structure of relationship; and then last, the word of God in Scripture preparing us for the Word of God in sacrament.

I don't know how much you have heard about the FOCUS organization I founded. Our mode of operation is to take four recent college graduates, train and equip them, and put them on teams in service at Newman Centers and chaplaincies around the country. Our staff become the staff members of the local chaplaincy. Their boss is the pastor or the chaplain and we are their coaches. The team's job is not to hang out at the Newman Center. In fact, at least in the early years, we did not want them to have an office in the chaplaincy because we wanted them out playing sports and hanging out with college students, cooking hamburgers, making hot chocolate—whatever it is that the students enjoy doing. We like to tell the team, "We want you to go on a campus, find college students and do everything they love to do that is moral!" Just go out and love them! Just love them. Just get in their lives and share life with them, become friends with them, because that is actually how God loved us. Before he invited or actually built the church, he came down to earth and lived with people. His mode of operation was to find twelve men and go camping for three years. He just invested deeply on a human level, on a relational level. And what happens in the midst of human relationships? Well, in the midst of human relationships, your friends become my friends and my friends become yours. That is how we meet people. We're not going to become friends with everybody in other people's lives, but if they are close to us, we will probably become close to those that are closest in their lives. If you are an intentional disciple of Jesus Christ, the most important relationship in your life is your relationship with God. That becomes an offer to share your closest relationship with other friends. Evangelization takes place before you ever get to church, and will also be what happens after we've been to church. It becomes a revolving spiral staircase that always is ascending and that spreads from one to another. We are starting in the field and we are saying we are just going to go out and love people where they are and invite them into relationship with us first and then with our closest friends.

Let's just step back because I think we sometimes have an allergy in the church, a nervousness about evangelization within the church. I get this comment all of the time: "Well, Curtis, you teach people how to evangelize, you are an evangelist, you serve on the Pontifical Council for the New Evangelization, you know about evangelization. We don't. We don't know how to do it. Would you come do a workshop for us, or maybe you could write a workbook for us and then we could go to the workshop and we can work through the workbook and then we would have some training in evangelization." I'm convinced that would help. But I'm also convinced that is not the issue. Let me give you an example. I come into town and I go to the finest restaurant in town where I have the best meal I have ever had. Then I see my friend Lynn and tell her all about this restaurant I went to last night. "The food was amazing, the ambiance was wonderful, and the pricing was great. This is a great restaurant, you have got to check it out." What I would not say is, "Gosh, if I can go to a workshop on how to share good news about restaurants, and maybe go through a workbook, then I would be qualified to tell Lynn about the restaurant." I wouldn't do that, right? The other thing I wouldn't do is turn to Lynn and say, "This restaurant is amazing and you have to go to it or you are going to hell!" I wouldn't do that either. Evangelization isn't either one of those. You don't need to have all the structure; you just need to share the Good News. And it isn't about judging someone on what they do with the Good News. That is between the person and God. Our only job is to deliver the Good News. If I don't deliver the good news to you and you wanted to go to a great restaurant and I knew about a great restaurant and the only reason you didn't go is because I never told you, that's bad on me.

I really believe that a huge part of why Catholics struggle with evangelization is not because we lack the training, but because the vast majority of Catholics do not experience their faith as Good News. It's a little bit more like fire insurance. "Well how's that Catholic thing going for you?" "Oh, it's going all right." "Are you going to quit?" "Oh, probably not." "Well why not?" "I don't want to go to hell." You've got some fire insurance going for you. I'm not excited about my insurance policies. I'm glad they are there because I might need them, but I don't get excited about it. A lot of people have a relationship with the Catholic Church that is kind of like our relationship with our insurance brokers. We are glad they are there; we don't get excited about it. The first step of overcoming apathy is just getting into people's lives. In the midst of that, you begin to share experiences.

I want to move into the liturgy. Now, I am not speaking as a priest. I'm a layperson so I am just going to share insights that come when we look at the liturgy as laypeople. The first thing I want to say is that the liturgy itself is amazing. The church teaches us *lex orandi, lex credendi*, the law of prayer is the law of belief. But I would argue that there is a veil that is over most Catholics' eyes. It's a veil of familiarity. They know the Mass so well, they don't know what they're looking at. I'll give you a couple of examples. One of the things I like to ask college students is, "Have you ever been at Mass and just intentionally prayed for everybody else in the church, that God would forgive their sins? Have you ever done that intentionally at Mass?" The reason I ask is because you are asked to do this, explicitly with the words "through my fault, through my fault, / through my most grievous fault; / therefore I ask blessed Mary ever-Virgin, / all the Angels and Saints, / and you, my brothers and sisters, / to pray for me to the Lord our God." But none of us actually does it. We are asked every time the *Confiteor* is prayed, but very few lay Catholics have ever sat back and said, "There are people in this room that are separated by sin from you, and I'm just praying now that you, Lord, would honor their presence here and forgive them their sin. Your Son has won this for them." There is a lack of engagement because, while it's what we are praying, it's not what we are thinking. I would argue that many of the Catholics in Washington, DC, might behave differently if they prayed the Creed and meant it. "I believe in one, holy, catholic and apostolic Church . . ." I'm not here to judge that one church. I'm here to stand as a child who looks at the church as a mother and teacher, and I should allow my conscience to be formed by her and have my values influenced by her, rather than me turning the tables around.

Or one more example is to recognize what we say to young people who are thinking about getting married. This is essentially what you do when you get married in the Catholic Church, within the liturgy, but it is a little bit veiled. You actually stand with God as your witness, the rest of the church as your witness, and an official of the church as a witness who is officiating the wedding liturgy. You look at the person you're marrying and you say, "I swear to God I will never cheat on you. I will never divorce you, and I will never contracept with you. I swear that before Almighty God." Now, the language is a little bit veiled and the bride and groom don't realize they are saying that. But, oh my goodness, it would be really important to know what they are pledging, wouldn't it? Actually, when it comes to addressing the validity of marriage we go right to those issues. They have said those vows in so many words.

One of the things we have done in our FOCUS team discussions outside of Mass with people is to break open the prayers. What I would advise you to consider, from time to time, is breaking open some of the prayers so that people can hear what they are saying with new ears. So much of the New Evangelization is helping people to take a new look at something they already own but have lost their appreciation for, to have that deepening, that awakening. The liturgy prayers are powerful, but we, as Catholics, need to get much more intentional about understanding what we are praying.

We have heard the old teaching, "no salvation outside the church." One of my priest friends asked me a question about that, and here's how I would answer it. In all four of the main eucharistic prayers we always pray for believers and nonbelievers who have died. It takes just slightly different forms, but we pray for all of our brothers and sisters, those "whose faith you alone have known." These are two different groups of people: all Christian believers, the Catholics, and everybody else that God knows. There is some form of this at every Mass for people who died who weren't members of the Catholic Church. If we believe in the absolute way that some of the ultraconservatives view "no salvation outside the church," why would the prayer be there? Why would it be there at every single Mass? The church is the normative way that God is effective, but he's not controlled by the sacraments. He has given them to us as tools for salvation. And if we know about them, we ought to use them. But for those who don't know, he honors that, he knows their hearts. I can't judge whether they will have salvation. I don't know, and neither do you. But in every prayer, there's always the hope for those who died outside of a formal relationship with the church, and that gives me great hope. It also gives me something more to pray about when I go to Mass. I become very intentional about that moment in the Canon because I have family members who are away from the church. I'm adopted and my birth mother wasn't Catholic. I can pray for her and everybody in her family. It's a beautiful thing to hope and pray with the church, with the priest, with the Eucharist, to be able to pray with great confidence with Jesus Christ to the Father for their salvation. The teaching sits around us in so many ways, but we are just overwhelmed by riches, and to open those up to people, bit by bit, can be a great tool. I know that it has brought great fruit in our work.

I want to focus now on the Scriptures. I will give a couple of examples from the Scriptures because I think the Scriptures are the primary mode of the encounter with Jesus Christ. I live in Colorado. I certainly have had moments of experiencing God's power while walking in the Rocky Mountains. As Archbishop Charles Chaput said, "We have two great cathedrals in Denver. One of them is man-made down in the city, Immaculate Conception, and one of them was made by God, just to the west." You can experience God in nature. You can experience God in relationship with other humans. You can experience God in an encounter with the sacraments. But the Scriptures hold pride of place and they hold pride of place in the Mass. There is only one book that has been read at Mass, and it has to be read at every Mass, and that is the Bible. All of the sacraments are made for one another. When lovemaking is done well within marriage, a couple spends time together and they share their hearts. They share conversation, and that conversation builds unity, which leads to a one-flesh union. The church has so orchestrated the liturgy that God would speak to his people, and they would break open the Word so that they would hear him more clearly so that they could then have a one-flesh union with Jesus Christ. This is an analogy that isn't a stretch; the book of Revelation makes it explicit.

How, then, do we look at the Scriptures? There are a couple of passages that the *Catechism of the Catholic Church* gives us right in the very beginning, just two tools that I'd like to share with you. We have had great experiences using these with tens of thousands of college students in small-group Bible studies, but these same principles can be unleashed in homilies and they flow right from the heart of the church. The first one says, "Be especially attentive 'to the content and unity of the whole Scripture'" (112).[1] Then it goes on to talk about reading Scripture from the heart of the church and the heart of Christ. This is a powerful sense of coming to know the Bible. And again, I don't think there has ever been a better time to learn the Scriptures than right now.

I don't know who your favorite teachers are, but I can tell you that I have worked with Scott Hahn, Jeff Cavins, Tim Gray, Edward Sri, and others and I believe they are unleashing a power in Scripture in some of the most wonderful ways I have ever seen. The feedback from their teaching is consistently that it is like the Emmaus Road encounter: "Were not our hearts burning?" I don't think it's because they are the greatest teachers on earth. I do think it's because they found one of the greatest teachings on earth and that is the metanarrative of salvation history. Our Protestant brothers and sisters know the verses. If you go to a football game and somebody holds up a sign that says "John 3:16," the evangelical says that is the Gospel in one verse: "For God so loved the world that he gave his only Son, so that everyone who believes in him might not perish but might have everlasting life." And Catholics look at the sign and say, "Some guy named John must have a birthday on March sixteenth." That's not our home game to know the Bible verses. Where Catholics do play great home team ball is, we know the stories. You can stand in front of a group of Catholic people and say, "There was a wealthy man who had two sons and the younger of the two came to him and said, 'Father, give me my share of the estate.' The father gave it to him, and what do you think he did?" They'll all say, "He squandered it." "And then what happened?" "He repented." "And then what happened?" "He came home." Catholics know the story. And if you say, "That's awesome; you know the story about the Prodigal Son! Where in the Bible is that?" "Uh, Lent?" They don't usually know. But here's the cool thing, it's in Luke chapter 15. It's so much easier to teach Luke chapter 15 than to teach the story. But neither verse knowledge, like our Protestant brothers and sisters have, nor story knowledge is what really changes your life. It is metanarrative knowledge that changes lives. When you know how the stories work together into a masterpiece that begins with God creating men and women walking through the fall and all of the problems that ensue, then seeing a God who passionately pursues his people first through his prophets and kings and then later through his Son, and continuing on through the ages even to now. To know God, because the metanarrative doesn't just tell us about God, it tells us who God is. Most modern people do not disbelieve in God.

They actually have a sense of God and are kind of freaked out by what they know about him. He's all-powerful, all holy, and probably a little angry, maybe more than a little angry. So they just ignore him because it's an unpleasant thought that he is angry and they don't know how to fix the problem. God's heart is on trial in the modern world. People don't so much doubt his existence; they doubt his goodness. Metanarrative speaks to the goodness of God and to be able to break that open and be attentive to the whole content of Scripture is beautiful.

The *Catechism* talks about the four senses of Scripture and how we can open that up (115). We have found tremendous value on placing emphasis on the literal interpretation. Of course you need to know the genre, you need to know the context, you need to know how those statements are used in other places in Scripture, so you have to have a growing knowledge of Scripture to do this well. One example, which is one of the simplest ones I can think of, is Matthew chapter 13, where Jesus gives seven parables about the kingdom. It's a wonderful, wonderful teaching, and each of them is very powerful, but my favorite one in some ways is actually the very shortest one of the entire chapter, and that is Matthew 13:44, a parable one verse long. In all of the parables Jesus is trying to stress some aspect about the kingdom, and in another setting when he talks about kingdom that means church. It means Catholic Church. We know this because it was very specific in that it was David's kingdom. If you go back and read Kings, all of David's sons had a prime minister. The prime minister possessed the keys to the kingdom. He was in charge when the king was gone and he ran the day-to-day affairs, even when the king was there. What did Jesus do, just before he turned his face toward Jerusalem to die? He appointed a prime minister and gave him the keys. There are only three times in Scripture that keys are mentioned: first, when the son of David is removing the keys from one prime minister to give to another; second, when Jesus hands the keys to Peter; and third, when we see Jesus possessing them fully at the end of all time. No need for a prime minister anymore—he is in charge. The other thing is in the kingdom of David, all of the sons of David, every one of those kings, had a queen, and it was never his wife. It was always their mother. The mother held an office, which was to sit in her son's throne room at his right hand and intercede for the people. That was her job. The term for this in Hebrew was *gebira*, or mother of my Lord, which is precisely how Elizabeth greeted Mary. "How is it that the mother of my Lord would come to me?" Jesus is talking about the church.

Back to Matthew 13:44, which is just a simple one-sentence, one-verse parable that talks about the kingdom of heaven being like a treasure hidden in a field that a man found and hid. Then, for joy over it, he went and sold all that he had and bought the field. I love to be able to wrestle with the literal sense to walk through that, because I think that Catholics can learn from the literal sense. I know I have. When I talk to Catholics and read this to them, they have actually heard it before. They know the story, but familiarity has blinded them, and they actually miss something really important. It's like you're talking to a basketball player late in the game who has grabbed his knees and is bent over breathing heavily and says, "This Catholic thing is tough. It's a lot of work. Doesn't it always feel like it is Lent to you?" But I go back to this passage and I think they are missing something. You talk to them a little bit more and you ask them, "Why are you working so hard?" "Well, I've got to do the right thing because I don't want to go to hell." But that's not what this verse says! They're trying to do the right things so that they can experience joy. But the verse says the discovery of the treasure brought joy first, and then the selling of the stuff happened when you already have the joy. Do you think the guy who found the treasure is walking around going, "Oh crud, I've got to sell my stuff." I don't think so! I think he is walking around laughing and asking people, "Want to buy a watch? How about a car? I will sell you anything, make me an offer—really, seriously, I'll sell you anything!" Because he knows as soon as he sells his stuff he can buy the field, and he wins! The joy comes first; we do this for the sake of the joy. In fact, we are told in Hebrews that Jesus could confront the cross because of this joy. This knowledge should be driving us, but I don't think Catholics are driven by joy. You can unpack this single verse, in lots and lots of different ways, to be able to sit back and say, "Have you ever encountered Christ, that treasure, hidden in a field? Have you ever encountered him?"

I do think in my experience that the term or the notion of personal relationship is still somewhat foreign to Catholics. But when you move to the discussion of an encounter with Christ, you are playing a home game. Catholics seem to respond to that language, in my experience. They will sit back and say, "I don't know that I've ever actually discovered the treasure of great price. I'm doing all of the right things because I want to play by the rules, but I do kind of have a fire insurance policy with God. And you're saying there is something more, that joy should be driving me because I've already found the treasure. Okay, I can do that."

Another example of encounter is in John chapter 1. I want to invite you to do something that we do all of the time in small-group studies, and I think it can also be done in homilies. I want you to invite young people or people of any age into your *lectio*. Let's do that as we look at John chapter 1. In John chapter 1, just to set the context, this is the very beginning of Jesus' ministry. Jesus has just been baptized by John the day before, and John has said "Behold, the Lamb of God, who takes away the sin of the world" and "He must increase; I must decrease." Two of John's disciples hear this and start to follow Jesus and are now becoming disciples of Jesus. In my mind, Jesus has been baptized the day before and the two disciples were there and saw the heavens open up. They saw Jesus and thought to themselves, this could be the real deal. In my mind, Jesus now gets up and is leaving. Jesus is walking and the two disciples are ten yards or so behind him. Jesus stops and looks back at the disciples, who turn and act like they are not following him. Jesus continues to walk a little farther and he turns around and they turn around, again pretending that they are not following him. Finally Jesus turns around and catches them following him. And Jesus says, "What are you looking for?" And they say to him, "Rabbi . . . , where are you staying?" Jesus says to them, "Come, and you will see." They come and see where he is staying, and they stay with him. It is about four o'clock in the afternoon.

I don't know what your experience in reading the Bible is. The Bible drives me nuts. It drives me nuts because the stuff I want in there doesn't seem to be in there and the stuff that I don't think needs to be in there is. Later in this gospel John is going to tell us that if everything Jesus said and did had been written down, all the books on earth would not have contained what he said and did. So this is a very, very redacted list of things and yet we know it's four o'clock in the afternoon. Really? That's going to help me somehow? Why do I need to know it is four o'clock? Let me demonstrate how frustrating this is. If you were to take a pin and put it right through four o'clock on this page, and turn back one page, you would be in the last chapter of Luke's gospel. Let me read you one other verse from Luke's gospel. First I'll set it up again: on the road to Emmaus, two guys are walking along and Jesus shows up. They don't recognize him and continue walking, and I can just imagine in my mind something like this: Jesus says, "How's it going?" "What do you mean how's it going? You're obviously coming from Jerusalem. Are you the only one on earth who hasn't heard? I mean we thought Jesus was the Messiah and on Friday they killed him. And today his body is missing." Jesus asks them to tell him more about it. It's about a six- or seven-mile walk; I don't know how far along they were, but I'm sure they have a lot of time to talk. In my mind, Jesus listens to them, and I think he just wanted them to pour out their hearts. "So tell me about the hopes you had," he says to them. And they just pour their hearts out.

Finally, after Jesus has heard what's in their hearts, we read this verse, Luke 24:27: "Then beginning with Moses and all the prophets, [Jesus] interpreted to them what referred to him in all the scriptures." There was not a single verse about what Jesus said. It's the greatest Bible study in the history of the world and there's not one sentence, but you turn the page and you are going to find out it's four o'clock. Who was doing the editing of this book? I mean, seriously, what could possibly be going on? It's so frustrating! Just give me a paragraph, Lord! But there is nothing! And the next day it is four o'clock! *Lectio* is about wrestling with God. And you wrestle and sit back and realize four o'clock has to be there for a reason. It's not who edited this book, the Holy Spirit edited this book. It's exactly what needs to be there, so why is it there?

After thinking about it, you start to realize that John's gospel is written after all the others. The Synoptics of Matthew, Mark, and Luke are written, and John has probably read them all. All of the apostles are dead. John is the only one left from the original Twelve and God lays on his heart, tell my story. And so John, with much prayer and the inspiration of the Holy Spirit, sits down and thinks, "All right, I am going to tell the story of Jesus." He goes back to the beginning. And what's not clear from John's gospel, but is clear from the other gospels, is that the two disciples of John the Baptist are Andrew and John. John writes, "I remember the day I had been following John the Baptist and John said, 'Behold the Lamb of God who takes away the sins of the world,' and then he tells us that he has to decrease and Jesus has to increase. Then John baptized Jesus, after a little bit of an argument, and the Holy Spirit descended upon him. The next day Andrew and I decide we have to follow this guy. I remember we started walking away from the Jordan and Jesus looked back and he asked us, 'What do you seek?' We asked him where he was staying and he said, 'Come and see.' And we stayed with him. I remember it like it was yesterday although it was sixty years ago, but my life completely changed at four o'clock in the afternoon. The question is, what is your four o'clock?"

Do we recognize that this is what drives Catholicism? If the question is asked why a person is Catholic, an answer might be, "because my parents are Catholic" or "because I was raised Catholic." But that is not the right answer. The real question is, if you had never been raised Catholic, why would you be Catholic? The only answer should be, because I've encountered Jesus Christ and he has changed my life! I remember my encounter with him took place at four o'clock, even though it was sixty years ago or twenty years ago. Because our young people and people of all ages have not had that encounter, they are unaware of how central that experience is to who they are, and they don't have a sense of what drives them to be disciples. They haven't experienced being a disciple by simply taking the Scriptures and breaking open their *lectio* and wrestling with God and seeing where he leads them.

Once you take the lens of encounter and look at the four gospels and the book of Acts in particular, it's actually just a series, five books of encounters. As you start thinking about the way the gospels are written, it is like Matthew, Mark, Luke, and John are sitting back and reminiscing. "Remember that time in the boat and Jesus wasn't there and the storm was going on and then he was walking across the water? That was crazy! And we were freaked out! Then he came into the boat and he said, 'Be still!' and the storm was over! I've got to write that down, that was awesome!" It is just one encounter after another encounter after another encounter, and it shaped who they were.

If you think about it, that is true for all of our relationships. It doesn't matter what relationship. Our relationships are defined by our encounters. If we have a series of great encounters with somebody we have a great friendship. If we have a series of wounding, painful encounters we have a wounded, painful friendship. Encounters define relationships. We don't remember all the moments in a relationship, but we remember the pivotal moments. I remember the night my future wife walked into my life. I don't remember every day she has been in my life, but I do remember that one. I remember months later, almost a year later, after lots of friendship, our first kiss. I don't remember every kiss we have had, but I remember that one. I remember standing in front of Almighty God, and pledging my life to her. I could have been like the Catholic I used to be, which was the burden Catholic, and I could have stepped back and looked at her and said, "Oh crud, I'm going to have to give up a lot of freedom to do this. This is probably the last woman I'm ever going to kiss. I'm going to have to call when I'm late. I'll probably have to change diapers!" All of which is true, but that is not what I was thinking. What I was thinking was, "If she doesn't figure out in the next two minutes that I am marrying way up, I win! I will gladly call, I will gladly change diapers! I just want to share my life with this woman! I love her because she's a treasure that I've discovered, and now I get to possess that treasure!" What a joy that is!

This leads me back to the last part of the Catechism. It's not just the literal sense, but it's the other senses of Scripture that help people to encounter Christ. Let's go back to the parable in Matthew 13, but we will look at it through another one of the spiritual senses. One of the ways we are to look at the Scriptures is through the eyes of Christ, and when we do that, we begin to realize something pretty powerful. That is, in Jesus' eyes we're the treasure hidden in a field, and for joy over us he sold all that he had so he could buy us. Because the greatest story of Christianity isn't how much we love God or even that we love God. The greatest story about Christianity is that God loves us, even on our worst day! Just crazy loves us! And that should inspire us to live well, but the living well part is not what makes the relationship. He just loved us while we were yet sinners!

I don't think most Catholics know that. Most Catholics see a God in their mind's eye sitting back saying, "Behave or you're going to hell!" And there is a truth to that, but it's a broken, lesser half-truth. If we don't behave, and if we do rebel and don't return, we may be separated from him forever, but the bigger truth is God wants us to know that while we are gone from him he loves us every day like a father. He will sit patiently waiting for us to come back. And when he sees us return, he will run to us because he loves us on our worst day. How do we know that he loves you and me on our worst day? Because he loved all of us on our worst day, when we killed the Son of God. Jesus looked at his murderers and turned to his Father and said, "Forgive them." This is a God with crazy love for us. This is really Good News, and when people own that, I think that the apathy issue will evaporate, and then we can teach them the faith because they will want to know.

Endnote

1. *Catechism of the Catholic Church*, 2nd ed. (United States Catholic Conference—Libreria Editrice Vaticana, 1997).

Chapter 7

The Bilingual Preacher, Catholic Social Teaching, and the Hispanic Community

David H. Garcia

In 1730 the king of Spain was anxious to extend his control over what is now Texas. Colonists were recruited from the Canary Islands to begin what would be the first civic settlement in the area. These islanders were poor families that had no idea where Texas was, much less about the challenging conditions of beginning a new life there. To entice them, the crown offered a plot of land and a title of nobility for each head of family. Both offers meant a lot to landless, impoverished people who had always lived on the margins of society. The title that would be conferred was "hidalgo." This referred to people who owned land. It is interesting to see where the title "hidalgo" comes from linguistically. Pulling the letters apart, they signify "hijo de algo" or "son of something," which almost seems humorous. What is the something? The more I have thought about it, to be a son of something is better than to be a son of nothing! It is the difference between seeing yourself as somebody or nobody.

The church needs to affirm that everybody is somebody in the eyes of God. We do that when we open the doors to welcome them in. Often the door has not been open to immigrants and people of different languages and cultures who come to our parishes. Maybe we just did not know how to open that door. The title of Pope Benedict's document on the New Evangelization is *Porta Fidei* or "Door of Faith." An open door and a welcome tell people they are somebody and they belong. We are called to keep that door open. Through that door is not only an encounter with Christ but also the subsequent call to be missionaries for Christ. Language and culture affirm and welcome people. As preachers these must be part of how we prepare our homilies. To use the language that is most familiar to the people with images, examples, and stories from their culture affirms the people and lets them know that they are important and they are very welcome in the church.

A very familiar saying or *dicho* in Spanish is *Mi casa es su casa* or "My house is your house." It conveys that total sense of welcome, warmth, and sharing that the stranger or visitor needs to hear in order to feel comfortable and at home. This attitude always needs to be what is communicated to everyone who approaches our churches. The goal, especially with immigrants and those of other cultural backgrounds, is to help them feel welcome and a part of the family so that they not only feel at home as they worship with the community but also begin to hear the call to ministry, leadership, stewardship, and mission. Pope Benedict, in his letter *Porta Fidei*, said of that door of faith, "To enter through that door is to set out on a journey that lasts a lifetime."[1] It is that sense that we convey to the one who comes to our parish church, namely, that they have come home to live and to stay.

There are forty-five million people in this country who speak Spanish as a first or second language. Many Hispanics in this country are bilingual, at least to some extent. There are Hispanics in the Southwest whose ancestors arrived there in the seventeenth, eighteenth, and early nineteenth centuries before those areas were part of the United States. They never crossed a border. Hispanics born in this country often do not have the fluency of speaking Spanish but still identify with the cultural images, stories, and traditions. To become successful preachers to this large and growing community, there is a need to become familiar with the culture and language of Hispanics, and integrate that into our preaching.

There are other bilingual Catholic communities of various ethnic and national groups in the United States. These reflections are offered from the Hispanic perspective with the hopes they could also provide some encouragement for preachers in other communities as well.

Catholic Social Teaching

Catholic social teaching is now front and center in the church, especially with Pope Francis's focus on becoming a "poor church for the poor." The pope is challenging the church to integrate this important part of our tradition into everything we do. He has often spoken directly about the need to improve our preaching and how we communicate this message.

Seven fundamental themes of Catholic social teaching are (1) the dignity of the human person; (2) rights and responsibilities; (3) the social nature of humanity; (4) the option for the poor; (5) the dignity of work and the rights of workers; (6) solidarity; and (7) care for creation. The popes and bishops have all applied these teachings to the many issues of our time through encyclicals, as well as other papal and episcopal documents, in fulfillment of their teaching authority. It is essential for the preacher to help people see these issues as part of the rich Catholic tradition of following the one who washed the feet of his disciples.

Bilingual Preaching: Two Homilies

Hispanics who have often suffered from poverty and discrimination yearn to hear the Good News. We preachers need to better understand how to reach them in our homilies. I contend that it is not acceptable to simply prepare a homily in English and then translate it into Spanish and fulfill our obligation to communicate the message to Hispanic people. The reason that a simple translation is not the way to go is that when one switches languages there is also a change of cultures. For example, generally speaking, the North American culture is more of an individualistic culture, while the Hispanic culture is more of a communally oriented culture. With a different culture come different meanings for words and phrases, as well as different images and stories meaningful to the people.

A preacher in a mixed congregation of Hispanics and others needs to prepare two homilies, which can be related or distinct. If the Mass is a bilingual celebration, then the preacher should preach two homilies within the same Mass, maybe six to eight minutes each. The first homily should be in only one language and develop as usual around one or more of the readings. Finishing that homily, the preacher then delivers the second one in the other language and could refer to another reading or reflect on the same readings as the first homily.

Some bilingual preachers prefer to speak English and Spanish in the same homily, at times switching languages every few sentences or even every few words. The result, in my opinion and experience, is confusion for those who are monolingual and irritation for those who are bilingual. Preaching two brief and culturally appropriate homilies is a respectful and good way to reach everyone in the congregation. Not every bilingual preacher would agree with me, but as one who has preached for over forty years and has also sat in many congregations listening to bilingual preaching, I feel this is the best approach. Monolingual people hear one culturally appropriate homily while bilingual people hear two. I have many people in bilingual Masses comment that they appreciate this style of preaching.

Emmaus: A Three-Step Homily

Preparing a homily is always a challenge no matter how long we have been preaching. I feel that a good preacher must begin with a prayerful reading of the Scriptures for the day and then allow the Scriptures to "percolate," as it were, inside of him for the days leading up to the preaching. This cannot happen without time. Over these days the readings will begin to deepen within us and we see and hear things in our lives, in the community, and in the world that these readings will speak to. The homily will slowly begin to come together as we include exegesis and more reflection. If we agree that preaching the Gospel is preeminent in our ministry, then we can do no less than to give it priority of time in our week.

The Emmaus story in the Gospel of Luke is a good model for preaching Catholic social teaching. The United States bishops, in their 2013 document about the Sunday homily, *Preaching the Mystery of Faith*, say that this story provides insights for our preaching. I feel it provides three steps that can inform our preparation. As the story begins, two disciples are leaving Jerusalem on Easter Sunday, discouraged about what had happened to Jesus, thinking that all their hopes about the Messiah were dashed with his death. The first thing to note is that they are leaving Jerusalem, which for St. Luke is the key place for the disciple to be. Throughout the gospel Luke tells us Jesus is heading toward Jerusalem and inviting those who want to be his disciples to carry the cross after him. Jerusalem is the place of the paschal mystery and disciples need to be there in the midst of it all. So, it is clear that something is wrong at the beginning of this reading.

In the Emmaus story, a stranger approaches to walk alongside the two travelers and they begin to converse. Luke tells the reader the stranger is Jesus but the two disciples do not know. Jesus begins by asking them what they are talking about, and they respond in surprise that anyone around the area would not have known what transpired there the past few days. Jesus asks them to tell him what is on their minds. *Step one* in preaching is to begin where the people are, not to begin where the preacher is. What is happening in the community, in the news, in their homelands from whence they come? The preacher needs to be aware of where people are and what they are thinking about and begin there. Pope Francis said at the chrism Mass of 2013, "Our people like to hear the Gospel preached with 'unction,' they like it when the Gospel we preach touches their daily lives." When we speak to the realities of their lives people listen, relate, and respond. After Holy Week last year, one of my parish members wrote me the following note: "You are truly blessed the way that you connect the readings and your homily to current events and how the word applies to today's living."

What are the realities happening in the Hispanic community of this country today, realities that form the base on which the Scripture of the eucharistic celebration shines? Certainly there are always family issues—the younger generation struggling between the Hispanic traditional mores and the pull of US secular society, the elderly and their place in the community, the stories coming from Mexico, the economic struggles to make a life for a family, and many other cultural issues. When we keep our ears and eyes attuned to what is happening in the lives of our community, there is always a rich treasure of material that the Scriptures can speak to.

As the Emmaus story continues, Jesus first listens to the two disheartened disciples and only then does he begin to shine the light of Scripture on the human condition that they have explained. Luke tells us Jesus begins with the prophets and other Scripture to show that what the disciples had related to him was supposed to happen to the Messiah. Later Luke tells us how these words caused their hearts to burn with excitement because Scripture had the answers they were so desperately looking for. *Step two* of our preaching is to let Scripture speak to the human reality. The preacher needs to let people see how often what happens in Scripture is what is happening again to them. We should see how the authors of the Scriptures went through much the same issues and problems in their communities that we face today. We can see how the colorful images of the stories in Scripture have power to speak to us in our situation. This can inspire us and begin to make sense for our lives today.

Finally, the two disciples arrive at Emmaus, but Jesus acts as if he were continuing on. They insist he stay with them, and it is at the table in the breaking of the bread that their eyes are finally opened and they recognize him. He vanishes, but they cannot contain themselves. They excitedly agree that their burning hearts in hearing the Scriptures and experiencing the breaking of bread and the presence of Jesus are telling them that they must return to Jerusalem to spread the Good News. They are now on the right path, namely, the road toward Jerusalem, the way of the disciple who follows Jesus in carrying the cross. Even though it is late, they do not wait since the proclamation of the Good News is always an urgent task.

The final step, therefore, of the homily is to address the question of what must be done in light of how the Scripture has illuminated our lives and stories and what we have experienced around the eucharistic table. Namely, what are our marching orders? In the third chapter of Luke the people listening to the powerful preaching of John the Baptist ask, "What then should we do?" in response to his preaching. The Baptist immediately answers, "Whoever has two tunics should share with the person who has none. And whoever has food should do likewise" (Luke 3:10-11). The homily, especially concerning the social teachings of the church, should motivate us to ask what we must do and how we must act. How do we respond to a brother or sister in need? Why are some social structures so unjust and hurtful to the poor? How do we address the terrible inequality in the world, where a billion people do not know if they will eat today while so many of us waste food constantly? How can I think globally and act locally? The homilist can help by giving some concrete suggestions for local action. The experience of hearing how Scripture and the sharing of Eucharist speak to the realities of our lives and call us to action is the basic goal of any homily.

The Hispanic Liturgical Calendar

In the Hispanic community there are special feasts and customs that are good opportunities to reflect on some of the social teachings of the church. I often incorporate these feasts or customs into the homily of the Sunday before or after the feast, since Sunday is the day most will be at church. It does not change the readings or the Sunday celebration, but merely adds a theme that the people will relate to and want to hear more about. Below are some examples of various annual feasts from the Mexican American cultural tradition beginning with the Advent season, and how themes from these could be developed in homilies.

1. *San Juan Diego, December 9*. Themes: indigenous people throughout the world and their rights, preferential option for the poor, solidarity.

2. *Our Lady of Guadalupe, December 12*. Themes: liberation from oppression, God chooses the lowly, preferential option for the poor. The banner of Guadalupe has been used during the Mexican Revolution of 1810 by

Fr. Miguel Hidalgo, the farmworker movement in the United States by Cesar Chavez, the pro-life movement, and the struggle for comprehensive immigration reform, among other social justice issues.

3. *Las Posadas, December 16–24.* The tradition of reenacting the journey of Joseph and Mary to Bethlehem searching for room at the inn and being rejected until finally finding the stable to give birth to the Messiah takes place in the barrios, streets, and on church properties. Themes: immigrants and immigration reform, refugees, and migrants throughout the world. There are over forty-five million forcibly displaced persons in the world today.

4. *Los Santos Inocentes (The Holy Innocents), December 28.* In 2014 over sixty thousand unaccompanied minor immigrants came to the United States from Central America escaping violence and poverty. Single mothers with children are the largest group in poverty and form the majority of refugees in the world. Themes: migration and refugees caused by violence, human rights of refugees, pro-life issues, child protection and neglect, child labor.

5. *Los Reyes Magos (The Magi, Epiphany), January 6 or Sunday after New Year's.* Themes: income inequality, fair trade, migrants.

6. *La Candelaria (The Presentation), February 2.* Hispanic traditions on this day involve taking babies born in the last year to church to be blessed as well as images of the baby Jesus from the home nativity scene. Themes: raising a family with dignity, educational inequality, division and separation of families due to immigration laws, healthy pregnancy, maternal and infant mortality, pro-life issues.

7. *Senor San Jose (St. Joseph), March 19.* Hispanic tradition on this feast is to share a meal with others at the *mesa de San Jose*, the table of St. Joseph. Themes: food insecurity and hunger (twenty thousand people in the world die daily of hunger and its consequences), poor nutrition and its impact on the ability of children to learn.

8. *Miércoles de Ceniza (Ash Wednesday).* The type of fasting the prophets call us to is freeing the oppressed, sharing bread with the hungry, and clothing the naked (Isa 58).

9. *Viernes Santo (Good Friday).* Traditions of *Siete Palabras* (the Seven Last Words) and *Pésame* (Burial Procession of Jesus and Sharing Sympathy with Mary). Themes: injustices to families in oppressive countries, violent conflicts throughout the world, displaced peoples, human trafficking, religious freedom, capital punishment.

10. *Fiestas Pascua (Easter).* Hispanic tradition of the *cascarón* (confetti-filled eggshell symbolizing new life). Themes: care for creation, life issues.

11. *Deiz y Seis (Fiestas Patrias or Independence Days), September 16.* This is a civic feast but can be a moment to speak of social teachings as well. Themes: freedom of speech and religion, safeguarding liberty, rights and responsibilities in the community, participation in society, advocacy.

12. *Día de los Muertos (All Souls), November 2. Ofrendas* or home altars honor the dead and favorite saints on this day, and many decorate the graves of their loved ones with flowers and food. Themes: rights and care for the elderly, honoring the values of our ancestors, capital punishment.

Latinos have their heritage from many countries and there will be other feasts that are celebrated in those countries to commemorate, but this listing gives an idea of how to develop themes and possibly bring them into homilies, other talks, intercessions, or bulletin notes. The readings from the Sundays will often lend themselves to one of the themes, and certainly mentioning the feast will bring an immediate interest from the Latino congregation.

Solidarity

Global solidarity is a theme Pope Francis speaks about regularly. Latinos in this country can identify with solidarity since Latino immigrants migrate to escape grinding poverty, violence, or other push factors in their home country. Latinos in this country have also experienced issues such as lack of equal opportunity in education, housing, and economic development.

Catholic social teaching has much to say to Latinos who come to our parishes week after week. I hope this reflection on preaching our wonderful treasure of Catholic social doctrine bilingually and biculturally has stimulated your imagination as a preacher. There is surely more than one way to reach people. Preachers are privileged to have a special opportunity during the Sunday Eucharist. Additionally, there are many other liturgical moments and many more times in pastoral ministry to proclaim these teachings in the Hispanic community. May God help us make the most of it all.

Endnote

1. Benedict XVI, *Porta Fidei* (Vatican City: Libreria Editrice Vaticana, 2011) 1.

Chapter 8

Preaching the Mystery of Faith
and the New Evangelization

Donald Senior, CP

The focus of this chapter is the recent statement of the US Conference of Catholic Bishops, *Preaching the Mystery of Faith*, and its connection to the New Evangelization.[1] This document, approved at the bishops' annual meeting in November 2012, is a strong reaffirmation of the ministry of the Word, particularly in the context of the Sunday Eucharist. It follows upon a previous statement on preaching issued by the Bishops' Committee on Priestly Life and Ministry thirty years ago, *Fulfilled in Your Hearing*, a text that has served the church well over the past few years and is used in many seminary courses on preaching.

But a lot has happened to the church in the United States in the past thirty years, and the time was ripe for the bishops to turn their attention once more to this central ministry of the church. The bishops cite such things as greater cultural diversity in the US church; the impact of secularism on our culture; the wounds caused by the scandal of misconduct on the part of the clergy; the fact that so many Catholics, particularly the young, are drifting away from the church; and, in particular, the fact that many Catholics appear to be ignorant of the church's teaching and its life-giving practices.

You will recognize that many of these conditions—some of which have resulted in a hemorrhage of Catholics from the church or at least a diminishment of involvement—has prompted the call for the New Evangelization, already sounded by Pope Paul VI but especially a strong message of John Paul II and Benedict XVI. The concern of the New Evangelization is not only the wider outreach of the church to the world, its primary responsibility, but also the stirring up of the faith of those already Catholic but who have strayed from the practice of their faith. Certainly Pope Francis has continued this outreach of the church both in his words and perhaps even more eloquently in his example.[2]

The bishops recognize that despite some waning of attendance at the Sunday Eucharist, the Sunday homily remains one of the most important personal encounters that the priest and deacon can have with our people. And for Catholics, participation at the Sunday Eucharist and hearing the preaching of the Sunday liturgy is where they most encounter the face of the church! Therefore, in our efforts to breathe new life into the church, invigorating our preaching ministry is key.

I want to concentrate first of all on the theology of the Word that stands behind the document, and some of its implications for our preaching ministry, including what the bishops' document calls a "spirituality" of the preaching ministry.

A Consistent Theology of the Word

One of the remarkable features of the post–Vatican II church regarding our reflection on the word of God is the strong and consistent mode of reflection on what is the ultimate foundation for the church's mission to proclaim the word of God. One can draw, in fact, a straight line from the Dogmatic Constitution on Divine Revelation, *Dei Verbum*, formulated near the very end of the Second Vatican Council in November 1965, through the formulation of the *Catechism of the Catholic Church* in 1992 in its reflection on the Creed (which in fact draws heavily on *Dei Verbum*), and on to Pope Benedict's post-synodal exhortation of 2010, *Verbum Domini*, and finally to the US bishops' statement *Preaching the Mystery of Faith*. This latter text draws on all of the above-mentioned documents in reflecting on the preaching ministry.

There is a common pattern in each of these documents as they reflect on the word of God and the church's mission to proclaim that word to the world. The formulation found in Vatican II's *Dei Verbum* is seminal. You may recall that this document underwent a complex and controversial process before it was finally approved by the council fathers.[3] The original schema proposed at the opening session of the council was rejected as being too abstract, too scholastic, and too rigid in its formulation. Then a *peritus* for the German bishops at the council, Joseph Ratzinger, said that the schema was "cramped" and essentially "a canonization of Roman school theology."[4] Pope John XXIII sought a solution to the sharp divisions among the council fathers by appointing a commission to work on the text, a commission cochaired by Cardinal Ottaviani and Cardinal Bea—each of whom represented polar opposite viewpoints about the document! Ultimately the document, benefiting from the educational and formative process of the council's intervening sessions, would be approved by a near unanimous vote in November of 1965 during the final days of the council.

The fundamentals of each of the subsequent statements I have referred to are already found in the council's dogmatic constitution:

First and foremost, *Dei Verbum* roots the ultimate origin of the word of God within the Trinity itself. The God revealed in the Bible and proclaimed in Christian tradition is a God who self-communicates, a God who is not self-contained but one who wishes to reveal himself to the world. In the mystery of the Trinity we affirm that the one true God is also totally relational—the very nature of God defined in an eternal dynamic of love among Father, Son, and Spirit. It is from this very life of God that the impulse to create and to be in relationship with the world springs. This is evident in the account of creation that begins the biblical saga in Genesis chapter 1. Through his all-powerful word, God creates the universe in all of its dimensions and in all of its beauty. Above all, God creates the human being, male and female, as the summit of creation and establishes a loving relationship with humans.

Secondly, the Bible portrays the human person, male and female, as made in the divine image (Gen 1:26), and, therefore, as capable, indeed destined, to respond to God. Thus, revelation is not an abstract notion about the transmission of truth but at its root is a relationship between God and the world he created. Made in the image of God, the human person has both the capacity and the destiny to respond to God, to be in relationship and communion with God. This is fundamental to the whole theology of the Word developed in *Dei Verbum* and continuing to the present day.

Thirdly, the God who creates the universe and the human being does not stay aloof from his creation but is involved, although mysteriously, in human history. The long and tortured saga of Israel presented in subsequent biblical history reflects this conviction. God is present, protecting Israel, admonishing it, forgiving it, carrying it forward often in spite of itself. Although the main focus of the Bible is on God's unique people Israel, it is also clear that the God of Israel is also the God of the nations and that the entire history of all peoples and of the universe itself is God's arena.

Fourthly, the culmination of human history and of the revealing word of God comes in the person of Jesus Christ, the Word made flesh and the definitive revealer of God's word to the world. Here *Dei Verbum* turns to the prologue of John's gospel for the characteristic biblical illustration of this conviction (John 1:1-18), as does Pope Benedict in *Verbum Domini*. The Word who is with God from the beginning is the Word spoken by God and perfectly expressing God's being so that the Word is God. This is the Word that arcs down into the created world and becomes flesh. In the flesh of Jesus Christ, the community sees the glory of God. Other key texts that fashion this conviction are found, for example, in the opening words of the epistle to the Hebrews: "In times past, God spoke in partial and various ways to our ancestors through the prophets; in these last days, he spoke to us through a son, whom he made heir of all things and through whom he created the universe, / who is the refulgence of his glory, / the very imprint of his being, / and who sustains all things by his mighty word" (Heb 1:1-3). Or the expression in Ephesians also cited by *Dei Verbum*: "In all wisdom and insight, [God] has made known to us the mystery of his will in accord with his favor that he set forth in [Christ] as a plan for the fullness of times, to sum up all things in Christ, in heaven and on earth" (Eph 1:8-10).

Finally, the Word embodied and made flesh in Jesus Christ, a word expressed in his teaching and compassionate healing, in his gathering of a community, in his giving of his life in the fullness of love, in his conquering of death, and in his return to communion with the Father for all time. This full articulation of God's Word of redeeming love for the world is now entrusted to the apostles and their successors and, indeed, to the entire Christian community. Fired by the Spirit of God sent upon the church by the risen and triumphant Christ, the apostolic church is commissioned to proclaim the word of God to the world and, in the spirit of that Word, to form communities of life gathered in the name of Jesus and destined to be witnesses to the "ends of the earth" of God's redeeming love for the world. Here is the ultimate basis and the dynamic power for the church's preaching ministry.

This is the sequence, from the first impulse of creation through the incarnation and on to the apostolic mission of the church, that is first articulated in *Dei Verbum*, succinctly repeated in the Catechism, and beautifully expanded upon in Pope Benedict's eloquent *Verbum Domini* that, taking its cue from the general synod of 2008, reflects on the role of Scripture in the life and ministry of the church. And this is the same biblical and doctrinal basis for the bishops' statement *Preaching the Mystery of Faith*.

Dei Verbum and the Pastoral Renewal of the Preaching Ministry

The purpose of the bishops' statement *Preaching the Mystery of Faith* is to support and help invigorate the church's preaching ministry, particularly in the setting of the Sunday homily. In so doing, it ultimately responds to the pastoral recommendations formulated by *Dei Verbum* over fifty years ago. Those recommendations that come at the end of the dogmatic constitution were extraordinary, urging the church to deepen its love of the Scriptures and to give them a central place in the church's mission. It recommended a series of initiatives: renewal of biblical scholarship among Catholics; new translations of the Scripture from the original languages and translations done in partnership with Protestants; new tools for studying the Bible and making it part of popular devotion; the encouragement of full access to the Scriptures on the part of the laity; making the Scriptures the core of our catechesis and our Catholic theology; and, hardly least, renewal of preaching focused on the Scriptures that would become part and parcel of the council's liturgical reforms, including the institution of the three-year Lectionary.

The US bishops' document makes two further important points about the Sunday homily that are worth our consideration.

1. The Sunday homily is an integral part of the Eucharist itself. The Liturgy of the Word and the Liturgy of the Eucharist together form the sacrament we celebrate. The word of God proclaimed in the Lectionary readings and the word of God made present in the eucharistic action should reinforce each other, with one throwing light and meaning on the other. The Sunday homily is the connection point between the two with the preacher striving to open up the meaning of the Word contained in the Scriptures for the faith and life of the people who have heard the readings proclaimed, and then, in harmony with the spirit and tone of the biblical message, enacting the eucharistic prayer and feeding the people with the Body and Blood of the Word Incarnate.

2. The Sunday homily is also an opportunity, based on the Scriptures proclaimed and in harmony with the atmosphere of prayer and worship intrinsic to the Eucharist, for the preacher to nourish the people's faith and to help them appreciate the beauty and meaning of the church's teaching. In this way, the Sunday homily also becomes part of the New Evangelization.

This is a sore point for some who feared that the bishops' new statement would push the homily in the direction of a doctrinal lecture or a catechism lesson. All one has to do is read the bishops' statement to see that is definitely not the case. The bishops are emphatic that the homily is not to be a lecture; it is proclamation of the word of God. But the statement also points out there is an art to good preaching that can make a clear and compelling connection between the vibrant beauty of the Word and crucial teachings of the church that in fact flow from that Scriptural basis. *Preaching the Mystery of Faith* gives several examples: allusion to the church's social teaching grounded in the many gospel accounts of Jesus' care for the poor and marginal; the church's doctrine of the incarnation amplified in the accounts of Jesus' compassion, forgiveness, and searching out of the stray and thus revealing the human face of God; the meaning of the Real Presence and the power of the Eucharist illumined by the resurrection stories and the risen Christ's promise to remain with us; the church's responsibility for the salvation of the world illustrated in the dynamic missionary words of Paul or the stories of the Acts of the Apostles. At times when the readings provide an opening, the preacher can also connect them with phrases from the Creed or parts of the eucharistic prayer in which the faith of the church is proclaimed.

Preaching with an eye to the New Evangelization—that is, with an eye toward illuminating and deepening the Catholic faith and identity of the congregation—does not subvert the purpose or tone of the Sunday homily but actually is in full harmony with it.

The Spirituality of Preaching

One of the special features of *Preaching the Mystery of Faith* is that it considers the spiritual implications of such a theology of the word of God for the one who is called to proclaim that biblical word within the preaching mission of the church. It also gives brief attention to the practical demands of preparing and delivering the homily toward the end of the document. But the focus in this statement, especially compared to the previous statement *Fulfilled in Your Hearing*, is much more on the spiritual discipline and habits of the heart required by the responsibility of preaching the word of God. This is a valuable dimension of the bishops' statement. I will not repeat all of that section of the document here, but allow me to offer a brief summary of this section and then zero in on some personal reflections on what the beauty and power of the Scriptures might require of us who are called to preach.

The bishops' statement points to four key qualities that flow from the responsibility of the preaching ministry. I think most of them are self-evident:

1. *The preacher is seen as a person of holiness.* There are two aspects to this. I think we all know it is hard to proclaim the Gospel with integrity and force if we ourselves are not wrestling with the meaning of the Scriptures in our own lives. I think over time our people sense this. We have to strive lifelong to be what we preach. The text refers to Jesus' challenge to the Pharisees for lacking integrity, for being in effect "pious frauds" who preach to others but don't live that way themselves. Secondly, the bishops call us to a spirit of prayer and reflection as the first essential step in preparing a homily. We need to reflect on the Word and what it means to us before we can really be ready to form a message for our people.

2. *The preacher is to be a person of Scripture.* I will say more about this in a moment, but here, too, is something self-evident, I think. This is a matter of a habit of the heart, immersing ourselves in the world of the Scriptures. Reading and praying the Scriptures should be an essential part of our daily prayer. I know that many priests and other preachers use the Lectionary and the upcoming readings of the day as their source of meditation as well as a means of preparation for preaching, and I think that is a salutary practice. The welcome appearance of several handy publications of the daily and Sunday Lectionary readings (often coupled with other prayers and the Liturgy of the Hours) has extended this salutary practice to the laity as well.

3. *The preacher is to be a person of tradition.* Here is another key dimension of our responsibility as preachers of the Word. We need to be steeped in the church's teaching and able to communicate it with conviction to our people. The preaching and teaching role of those authorized to proclaim the Word remains key. *Dei Verbum* and subsequent Catholic reflection on the Word emphasizes the essential unity of Scripture and tradition, the one word of God expressed both in Scripture and in tradition.

4. *The preacher, the bishops emphasize, is to be a person of "communion."* It is significant that the bishops' statement spends more time on this than on the other qualities. The term "communion" is one framed by Pope John Paul II in speaking of the ministry of the priest in general. He was referring to the need for the pastor to love and respect God's people and to be in touch with their everyday experiences. This demands an awareness of what is happening in our world and sensitivity to and respect for the diversity of cultures that mark virtually all Catholic parishes today. The pulpit is a privileged and public place, and those who preach need to be aware of how they speak, even in passing, about other groups or other religious traditions. We can recall, for example, Jesus' exhortation to his disciples not to despise the "little ones" in the community (see Matt 18:10). Here the text is referring not to children but to those whom some might consider the insignificant and sometimes wearying members of the community.

Allow me to add one more reflection about the spirituality of preaching that is not explicitly noted in *Preaching the Mystery of Faith* but I think reflects its spirit as well as Pope Francis's remarks about preaching found in his beautiful exhortation *Evangelii Gaudium* (The Joy of the Gospel). Preaching with a biblical character should be expansive, evocative, and visionary rather than didactic, moralistic, or trivial. Preaching is, in fact, an expression of the essential missionary character of the church.

If the homily is to match the scope and character of the biblical text, and harmonize with the deep seriousness of the liturgy itself, then it should truly inspire and enlarge the Christian heart of the one who hears it. This is the spirit of the church's mission to the world, the call to proclaim the word of God, which is a word not of condemnation but of life, a word embodied and most vividly proclaimed in the person and mission of Jesus who is the taproot, the wellspring, of all Christian ministry, of all sense of mission.

When we use the term "mission" today, we mean it of course not just in the sense of mission *ad gentes*: in the image of the missionary leaving home shores and bringing the word of the Gospel to those who have never heard it. This dimension of mission remains valid, but there is also a more pervasive and all-encompassing sense of mission. In speaking of the commitment to mission on the part of those in consecrated life, John Paul II noted that the Christian "has the prophetic task of recalling and serving the divine plan for humanity, as it is announced in Scripture and as it emerges from an attentive reading of the signs of

God's providential action in history. This is the plan for the salvation and reconciliation of humanity."[5]

When considering our mission of proclaiming the word of God, no matter what the particular modalities of our ministry might be, we must keep in mind that the object of God's word is the transformation and salvation of the *world*. When I was in graduate school in Louvain, Belgium, I took a trip with a few friends to London to buy books, which were much cheaper there than on the continent. At Blackwell's famous bookstore in Oxford, I found a table that contained used books, each being sold for one pound. I was thrilled to discover a leather-bound edition of J. C. Hawkins's book on the Synoptic Problem, entitled *Horae Synopticae*.[6] Not bedside reading, for sure, but for an eager graduate student, truly a find! On the ferry on the way back I pulled out the book and saw that the original owner had penned an inscription in Greek in the frontispiece. It read, *ho de agros estin ho cosmos*. "The field is the world." Where was this quote from, I wondered? One of the ancient Greek poets? Only later did I realize, to my embarrassment, it was from the Gospel of Matthew (13:38), where Jesus explains the parable of the wheat and the weeds to his disciples! (I had been working on Matthew's gospel for my dissertation for many months!) The seed of God's word, Jesus says, is directed to the *world*. The focus of mission is not the church, not our domestic disputes, but the transformation of the world in all its glories and anguish.

Remember what is perhaps the most famous quote from the council? "The joys and hopes, the grief and anguish of the people of our time, especially of those who are poor or afflicted, are the joys and hopes, the grief and anguish of the followers of Christ as well. Nothing that is genuinely human fails to find an echo in their hearts. For theirs is a community of people united in Christ and guided by the holy Spirit in their pilgrimage towards the Father's kingdom, bearers of a message of salvation for all of humanity. That is why they cherish a feeling of deep solidarity with the human race and its history."[7] And if we are to proclaim the word of God to this world and in this church, we must have empathy for our world. The word of God is always incarnate at a particular time and place; it is not abstract or unchanging. I am struck how in the Scriptures themselves, the word of God and the mission to proclaim that word are so woven with human modalities. We often discover the meaning of our mission to the world only in the light of current events. To put it another way, mission is shaped not just by the forceful ideals and dreams revealed in the teachings of the Old and New Testaments but also by the mysterious stirrings of the Spirit alive in the world, shaping and moving among what may seem to be secular or impersonal realities in history. In fact the entire biblical saga reminds us that the Spirit of God is not confined to Israel or to the church but roams the world and works through events and people we might never anticipate.

This sense of openness to our world, in sympathy with its struggles and anguish, even as we are alert to its false values and wary of its se-ductions, is what the bishops' statement—drawing on the reflections of John Paul II, who used this term in speaking of the priesthood—says it means to be a person of "communion." To be aloof from our world, to take only a moralizing, negative stance toward our world, is not the spirit of Christ nor does it reflect the tenor of the biblical word.

I have been struck by the frequent comments of Pope Francis along these lines. For the church's face to the world to be only negative and corrective rather than radiating a sense of tenderness and care for our world, for the church to be absorbed only with its own life and concerns and not turned to the world, is, as the pope put it, to risk choking on its own stale air.[8] He himself repeatedly uses images of the church as mother, as nourishing, as tender and loving, as merciful, as reaching out particu-larly to the most vulnerable.

For most of our Catholic brothers and sisters, the face of the church will be most readily and frequently experienced in the words and atti-tudes projected in the Sunday liturgy and most intensely in the Sunday homily. The biblical word with which we are entrusted, the biblical word that is the word we proclaim, impels us to open our hearts in compassion and love for our people and for the world where God has placed us.

Imbibing the beauty and power of the biblical word itself, drawing on experience but not putting the focus on ourselves, being charged with the missionary spirit of the biblical word and having it shape our rela-tionship to our world—these are some of the ways that taking to heart our call to preach the biblical word will affect our spirituality.

Conclusion

The bishops' statement concludes with words of encouragement. As priests and people close to the church we are well aware of our problems: the corrosive and demoralizing effect of the sexual abuse crisis that continues to be a burden; the sense of diminishment that shrinking numbers and scarce financial resources inflict on us; the polarities and struggles of our society that also have an impact on the church. The list can go on. Some of these things we cannot control even as we struggle to live lives of integrity. Yet some things we can control. We can give new life to our preaching. We can work harder at our preparation. We can strive in our prayer and study to sink more deeply into the beauty and power of our Scriptures. We can remind ourselves and keep conscious of the fact that the ministry of preaching, particularly in the context of the Sunday Eucharist, is going to probably be the most important encounter we as priests and ministers of the Gospel have with our people, and for our people that same Sunday homily is probably their most important encounter with the living word of God and with the face of Christ's church.

We all have different personalities, different backgrounds, different experiences, different capacities for public speaking, different styles of preparation and of delivery. For some the preaching task may come fairly easy; for others it may be a constant struggle. But each of us—commissioned as we are to preach the Gospel, standing as we do in a long and noble tradition, rooted as we are in power of God's Spirit, and nourished as we know we are by the word of God—can strive to proclaim the Gospel with more depth and beauty and power.

The bishops conclude their statement on preaching with a dedication to Mary. They cite the beautiful image of Ephrem and Augustine, that Mary first conceived the Word in her heart before conceiving the Word in her womb. We, too, like Mary the Mother of Jesus and the first proclaimer of the Word Incarnate, can strive to bear Christ in our hearts and in our words for the sake of the world.

Endnotes

1. US bishops, *Preaching the Mystery of Faith: The Sunday Homily* (Washington, DC: USCCB, 2013).

2. See, in particular, *Evangelii Gaudium*. Note that Pope Francis gives expansive and detailed attention to the role of preaching in the New Evangelization; see nos. 135–59.

3. See the discussion of the process in Ronald D. Witherup, *Scripture: Dei Verbum*, Rediscovering Vatican II (New York: Paulist Press, 2006), 1–31.

4. Glen Argan, "Constitution on Revelation Born with Labour Pains," *Western Catholic Reporter* (May 26, 2014), http://www.wcr.ab.ca/VaticanII/tabid/231/entryid/5475/Default.aspx.

5. John Paul II, *Vita Consecrata* (Vatican City: Libreria Editrice Vaticana, 1996) 73.

6. J. C. Hawkins, *Horae Synopticae*: originally published at Oxford by Clarendon Press, 1909.

7. Austin Flannery, ed., *Gaudium et Spes* 1, in *Vatican Council II: Constitutions, Decrees, Declarations; The Basic Sixteen Documents* (Collegeville, MN: Liturgical Press, 2014). *Preaching the Mystery of Faith* cites this same quotation in speaking of the preacher as a person of "communion"; see USCCB edition, p. 36. Pope Francis himself has repeatedly appealed to this same quotation in various public addresses.

8. See Pope Francis, letter to the Argentine bishops, April 18, 2013, http://en.radio vaticana.va/storico/2013/04/18/pope_mission,_the_best_cure_for_the_church/en1 -683985.

Chapter 9

Evangelizing US Latinos in the Twenty-First Century: Realities and Possibilities

Hosffman Ospino

> The preacher also needs to keep his ear to the people and to discover what it is that the faithful need to hear. A preacher has to contemplate the word, but he also has to contemplate his people. In this way he learns "of the aspirations, of riches and limitations, of ways of praying, of loving, of looking at life and the world, which distinguish this or that human gathering," while paying attention "to actual people, to using their language, their signs and symbols, to answering the questions they ask." . . . Preparation for preaching thus becomes an exercise in evangelical discernment, wherein we strive to recognize—in the light of the Spirit—"a call which God causes to resound in the historical situation itself. In this situation, and also through it, God calls the believer."
>
> —Pope Francis, *The Joy of the Gospel* 154

What an exciting moment to be a Catholic in the United States! Our shared experience of faith in more than seventeen thousand Catholic parishes spread throughout the country, with its ups and downs, is testimony that God continues to make wonders in our midst. As I travel around the country learning about how Catholics live and celebrate their faith, particularly Latino Catholics, and documenting such experience through research, I observe two common trends. On the one hand, many Catholics dwell in what I would call a "tent of disenchantment and lament" in response to major setbacks that have severely impacted the US Catholic experience in recent decades. Among such setbacks we can name recent moral and administrative scandals, financial hardships, massive defections, the closing of thousands of parishes and schools, the aging of communities, painful ideological battles that undermine ecclesial communion, and the growing influence of secularism among our young people, to mention only a few. Often people express the desire to return to some form of past and glorified Catholic experience, but soon realize that history only moves forward. Some seem to have lost hope in something better and thus embrace attitudes of indifference, retreat, even despair.

On the other hand, many Catholics in the United States dwell in what I would call a "tent of patient hope waiting for the right time to be protagonists." Here we find millions of immigrant Catholics who during the last five decades have profoundly transformed the face and culture of Catholicism around the nation. Their children practically constitute the majority of Catholic youth and young adults today. In this group we also encounter young women and men of all racial backgrounds who grew up in Catholic homes and are familiar with the best of Catholic values. We know that most of them are not actively involved in parishes, do not attend our Catholic schools and universities, and are not leaders within our structures. These young Catholics are raising families while discerning whether Catholicism will be central in that important task. For many of them, as well as for many immigrants, Catholicism is still the *de facto* matrix shaping their religious imagination. Yet, they live in the margins of our church. The question is whether they will wait any longer for the church's evangelizing efforts to reach out to them in a convincing manner and whether they will be invited to assume a protagonist role in their communities in light of their gifts.

The above categories give us some light into the context within which US Catholics are called to advance the New Evangelization in the twenty-first century. Like all categories, these are abstractions that seek to name a complex reality; other categories could certainly be added to the analysis. The point, nevertheless, is that the US Catholic experience is far from being homogeneous or static. We live in a very diverse church. If you were born in the 1950s, most likely you have witnessed major transformations in the US Catholic world during your lifetime. By the middle of the twentieth century, about 95 percent of all Catholics in the country were Euro-American white. Today, approximately 40 percent of US Catholics are Latino, 5 percent Asian and Pacific Islander, 4 percent black, and 1 percent Native American. The percentage of Euro-American Catholics has declined almost by half. The striking dynamic here is the remarkable growth of the nonwhite population, both in the church and in the larger society. Hispanics, for instance, "account for 71 percent of the growth of the Catholic population in the United States since 1960."[1]

Technically we all are part of cultural and racial minorities that together form the Catholic Church in the United States. During the second part of the twentieth century, the national parish system basically came to an end. There was no more need for parochial segregation according to nationality or language. Nonetheless, in the last four decades US Catholicism shifted into an almost *de facto* bilingual experience in which English and Spanish became indispensable to minister to large blocks of Catholics in the country—not to mention other common languages such as Portuguese, Vietnamese, Haitian Creole, and Tagalog. About 40 percent of all Catholic parishes in the nation are "shared parishes" or "multicultural parishes," meaning that they celebrate Mass in a language other than English and their populations are racially diverse.[2]

As the church in the United States grows in diversity in terms of culture, race, and ethnicity, it is important to observe that the socioeconomic conditions that shape the lives of Catholics throughout the country are changing rapidly as well. After World War II, a large sector of Catholics in the United States became highly educated, professional, and financially successful. The church as an institution benefited significantly from this growth, particularly in the structuring of worship, processes of faith formation, social outreach initiatives, and ecclesial administration. Today, most Catholic immigrants from Latin America, the Caribbean, Asia, and Africa in our churches struggle with poverty and low educational achievement. Only a small percentage is part of the professional workforce. Many of their children seem to be caught up in a world of circumstances that make social mobility and cultural integration more difficult. It will take more than one generation for these new Catholics to make the appropriate transitions in our society to succeed. This takes time. US Catholicism is transitioning from a modus operandi that fit well middle-class standards of being a church to one that must take into account a growing cultural and linguistic diversity, urban life, poverty, limited resources, and major educational needs at all levels.

In which tent do you dwell? That of "disenchantment and lament," or that of "patient hope waiting for the right time to be a protagonist"? Perhaps in between these two? A totally different one? Regardless of where we see ourselves as Catholics in the United States of America, the truth is that we have a responsibility as baptized Christians: announce the good news of Jesus Christ. Every generation of Catholics must proclaim, in season and out of season, that the Lord is risen and that salvation comes from God. We all do it in the midst of the sociohistorical context in which we are called to exist. This is our context. It is fine to experience disenchantment and lament. These feelings remind us that we can do better. The New Evangelization must bring a sense of hope and new life while inviting us all to trust more firmly in God's wisdom. It is fine to wait with patient hope for the right time to assume our protagonism. We know that our vocation is to be witnesses of Christ here and now. The New Evangelization must be an opportunity to creatively build community in new ways, listen to new voices, explore new approaches to ministerial life, and make way for those who are ready to take the lead.[3]

The church's evangelization efforts in the twenty-first century will flourish insofar as all Catholics understand the questions and meet the hopes and needs of the various groups that constitute the church in this country. Hence the need for what Pope Francis calls "evangelical discernment."

Turning Our Attention to Latinos Now

Where to begin? Preachers, educators, and evangelizers would do well engaging any of the sectors described above. But I would like to make a recommendation. Perhaps the most influential factor reshaping the US Catholic experience in the United States in the early part of the twenty-first century is the sociocultural and religious impact of the Latino presence in our Catholic communities across the United States.[4] Data from the recent *National Study of Catholic Parishes with Hispanic Ministry*,[5] for which I had the privilege of serving as the principal investigator, provides important insights. The study serves as an important instrument for planning Catholic ministry in the United States, making the church's evangelizing efforts more in sync with the needs and realities of the church at the grassroots level.

As noted earlier, Latino Catholics account for 71 percent of the growth of the Catholic population in the United States since 1960. The two main reasons stimulating the growth of Latinos are immigration and high birth rates. Currently, more than twenty million immigrants from Latin America and other Spanish-speaking countries live in the United States. Between 60 and 70 percent of these immigrants are estimated to be Catholic. Most of them are raising their children as Catholics, building on the cultural and religious values that they bring from their countries of origin while negotiating important elements of their identity as members of a new society where Catholicism is a minority religion and secularism is significantly influential. Rooted in traditional values of family life and community, most Latino immigrants pass on the faith to their children at home, usually in Spanish. Much of the evangelization process in the family occurs via practices of popular Catholicism such as *Posadas*, *altarcitos*, processions, *padrinazgos*, *quinceañeras*,[6] and particular devotions that often reflect the national origin of each community.[7]

Most often we encounter Latino Catholics in the context of parish life. Whether immigrant or US-born, active Latino Catholics normally search for a parish community to participate in the church's sacramental life, particularly the celebration of the Eucharist. In the United States nearly 4,500 parishes celebrate Mass and other services in Spanish, a number that continues to grow.[8] The Latino presence is positive for parish life. Parishes where Latino Catholics are present have larger numbers of people attending Mass, more baptisms, and more children enrolled in catechetical initiatives.[9] These parishes tend to be vibrant because of the large number of young Latinos and their families. Latinos in general are a young population. The median age of Latinos in the country is twenty-seven, compared to thirty-seven for the rest of the population. As indicated in the first report emerging from the national study, "Hispanic ministry in parishes is essentially ministry with youth and young families."[10]

When we look at the entire US Catholic population, we know that about 40 percent is Latino. But if we look at these numbers according to age brackets, the data is even more revealing: more than 55 percent of all Catholics in the United States under the age of thirty, and about 60 percent under the age of eighteen, are Latino. The present and future of Catholicism in our country is intimately linked to how we embrace young Latinos and respond to their questions and needs as part of the New Evangelization. But to do this, we must understand who Latino Catholics are in our day. We will return to this point in the next section of this chapter.

In the past pastoral care of Latinos was left largely to the initiative of Latinos themselves or pastoral leaders with a special interest in this population. Given the size of this group and its increasing influence in the life of the church, in the twenty-first century the pastoral care of Latino Catholics, particularly the young, is everyone's responsibility. The rapid growth of the Latino Catholic population challenges existing structures of service and evangelization that Catholics set in place in previous decades. Most of these structures are located in the Northeast and the Midwest. However, most Latino Catholics live in the South and the West—about two-thirds. For instance, 61 percent of all Catholic parishes are in the Northeast and the Midwest, thus leaving the regions of the country where Catholicism is growing fastest with less than 40 percent of all parishes to meet their needs.[11] Something similar occurs with Catholic schools and universities. They are vastly concentrated in those regions where Catholicism is presently not experiencing much growth. As we move along the twenty-first century, Catholics in the United States, in the context of the New Evangelization, will need to enter into a process of better sharing of limited resources while building more structures, particularly parishes and educational institutions, in those regions where Latino Catholics are present.

According to the Mode of the Receiver

Let us look closer at the experience of Latino Catholics as we affirm the urgency of increasing our evangelizing efforts toward this group in the life of the church in the United States. When asking Catholic parishes and dioceses throughout the country about their efforts to reach out to Latinos, it was interesting to observe that the vast majority of pastoral leaders working in these ecclesial entities defined "Hispanic ministry" as ministry primarily with Spanish-speaking Catholics.[12] This use of "Hispanic ministry" immediately raises a red flag. On the one hand, it gives the impression that the majority of Latinos in the country are immigrants, primarily Spanish-speaking. On the other, it points to the limitations of capturing the complexity of the US Latino experience with all-encompassing terms.

Aware of the complexity of the US Latino experience, it is important to make some clarifications. One, the vast majority of Latinos, 61 percent (nearly two-thirds!), was born in the United States. Two, most Latinos are English-speaking and conduct most everyday business in this language. However, most retain Spanish primarily at home. Three, while nearly two-thirds of Spanish-speaking immigrants from Latin America and the Caribbean self-identify as Catholic, the percentage drops significantly among US-born Latinos: 48 percent.[13] Let's keep in mind that 93 percent of Latinos under the age of eighteen were born in the United States. Also, as indicated above, about two-thirds of all Catholics under eighteen are Latino.[14]

What do we learn from these observations as we reflect on evangelization and preaching among Catholics in the United States of America in the twenty-first century? Perhaps the most significant insight from this discussion is the need to determine our evangelizing strategies in light of the needs and questions of multiple Latino audiences that we will encounter in our parish communities. Students of theology and philosophy, as well as Catholic educators and preachers, most likely have encountered Thomas Aquinas's principle, *quidquid recipitur ad modum recipientis recipitur*: "whatever is received into something is received according to the mode of the receiver."[15] The principle is normally interpreted from an epistemological perspective, arguing about the ability of the knowing subject to know a particular object that in turn is knowable. What receives little discussion is the role of context in shaping the process of knowing reality. In other words, once we have determined that it is possible for us to encounter the God of revelation here and now, understand the divine plan of salvation through the person of Jesus Christ, and assert the role of the believing community in mediating what is necessary for a relationship with the triune God to be truly life-giving, we need to ask what the questions are that people ask, or need to ask, in light of the particularity of their context for those true convictions to make full sense in their lives!

The New Evangelization in the United States definitely invites us to announce the good news of Jesus Christ with "new ardor, new methods, and new expressions." Most preachers and evangelizers would want all Latino Catholics living in the United States to strengthen their relationship with the Lord and become actively involved in the life of the church. God's Holy Spirit no doubt will continue to guide the church in this process. However, we must do our part. One of the most influential factors determining the success of the New Evangelization in the United States will be how well we engage the questions and respond to the needs of Latino Catholics. In order to do this, we must have a good sense of the various contexts in which distinct US Latino Catholic populations are discerning their religious experience. This is certainly a conversation that deserves an in-depth treatment beyond these lines. For now, let us delineate three interrelated populations and a few evangelizing needs.

Latino Immigrant Catholics

The most familiar group in the context of ministering to Latino Catholics is that of immigrants. This is a group that is easy to identify primarily because of the use of the Spanish language and the strong cultural ties to their countries of origin. Religiously speaking, most Latino immigrants hold on to traditional expressions of popular Catholicism, are familiar with official church practices, and are the population most likely to be present in parishes. While many are educated and arrived with the possibility of advancing professional careers or business opportunities, the majority lack formal education beyond the high school level and are affected by the reality of poverty. Millions live in the country as undocumented immigrants.

Evangelization efforts toward this group need to build on the wealth of cultural and religious experiences that they bring, usually shaped by the strong influence of Catholicism in Latin America and the Caribbean. Spiritual outreach often is to be combined with social outreach in the form of advocacy, basic education opportunities (e.g., English as a foreign language classes), human services, and political empowerment to participate as active members of the society to which they now belong. Preaching the Good News to this group cannot ignore the everyday struggles of these people. Some experience painful biases such as racism and classism. As immigrants they have left relatives, land, and culture searching for new opportunities. In the process of reinventing themselves in a new society, the church plays not only the role of an institution with which they already are familiar but also one that is expected to accompany them on a lifelong journey. Hence the need of building hospitable communities of faith where Christ is constantly welcomed in the newcomer, communities that Catholics from other nations and cultures can call home.

US-Born Latino Catholics

The largest body of Latinos in the United States is that of those who were born and raised in the country. Yet, traditional pastoral approaches to ministry have somewhat rendered them invisible. Attention to the immediate needs, questions, and challenges of Latino immigrants often create the illusion that US-born Latinos have exactly the same needs, leading to one-size-fits-all approaches even within Hispanic ministry. These approaches often evolve alongside pastoral practices that tend primarily to the needs of immigrants in a segregated manner, thus assuming that their children and grandchildren will benefit from them by default. At the same time, it is not unusual that these Latinos are also expected to "assimilate" into mainstream communities and practices because they are more comfortable speaking English and know better the culture in which they live. Yet, evangelization and inculturation are more than language and citizenship. Culture plays a major role in this process. One important case study in Catholic parishes is youth ministry with Latinos. It is interesting to observe that Latinos usually do not join mainstream parish youth groups in large numbers. Immigrant young Latino Catholics find themselves comfortable in youth groups conducted in Spanish, usually constituted by other youth from a similar country or region (e.g., Central America, the Caribbean). But US-born Latinos must decide between mainstream groups and immigrant groups. Culturally they seem to be able to negotiate better with immigrant groups, yet linguistically and socially their reality is different. While bilingual groups may seem a desirable temporary alternative, the alternatives are not that many.[16] To this we must add that investment in Hispanic youth ministry, particularly in terms of leaders and resources, is very minimal, almost nonexistent in most parochial communities.

Evangelizing efforts among US-born Latinos demand that pastoral leaders make the best effort to understand the complexity of being Latino in the United States. Besides the ethnic and cultural *mestizaje* that characterizes the experience of women and men living in between cultures, there are sociopolitical realities both in the church and in the larger society that often exacerbate the experience of Latinos. Millions of US-born Latinos—many of them Catholic—are trapped under conditions of poverty, low educational attainment, and lack of professional development. Many live in at-risk circumstances, which is often reflected in the high number of Latinos incarcerated throughout the country. Evangelization among US-born Latinos, particularly those who struggle the most in our society, must be an opportunity to bring a message of hope. To preach the Good News to this population requires continuous reference to a message of freedom and opportunity, affirmation and empowerment.

In the process of building communities that are welcoming to US-born Latinos, it is imperative to implement pastoral practices and evangelization strategies that highlight the fact that God walks with us in the in-between, that the God of life accompanies us in the struggles of the everyday. US-born Latinos today constitute the core of the generation of Catholics that will likely define the strength and vitality of the church in the United States in the first part of the twenty-first century. This is a generation waiting for an opportunity to take the lead, to be prepared and empowered to do so; it is a generation called to build upon what has been inherited, taking our faith communities into fresher waters. Are we ready for them? Do we support them? Do we believe in them?

Inactive Latino Catholics: Immigrant and US-Born

Taking care of the pastoral and spiritual needs of Latino immigrants and US-born Latino Catholics in our parishes as part of the New Evangelization is in itself a major task. However, these somewhat active Latino Catholics are merely 40 percent of the entire Latino Catholic population in the country. We are still left with 60 percent of Catholics who do not participate in Mass on a regular basis and are among the most likely to stop self-identifying as Catholic. Perhaps this is the most urgent commitment as part of the church's evangelizing mission in its service to Latino Catholics. The truth is that many of these Catholics will not wait long. It is estimated that one out of four Latinos in the United States is a former Catholic. The three most common reasons identified by Latinos who are former Catholics for leaving the church are: (1) gradually drifted away; (2) stopped believing in religion's teachings; and (3) found a congregation that reaches out/helps members.[17] Isn't the first step in the process of evangelization to reach out to the other in an invitational manner? Should we not open our communities to all Catholic brothers and sisters to experience the transforming love of Christ in the Eucharist and in the beauty of his Word? Perhaps the New Evangelization should be an excuse to do this in a much better way.

Shifting religious affiliation is increasingly common among young Latino Catholics. Latinos between the ages of eighteen and twenty-nine with more than a high school degree seem most likely to stop self-identifying as Catholic. When Latino Catholics stop self-identifying as such, some join other Christian groups, yet most become nonreligiously unaffiliated. This is more common among US-born Latinos.[18] Once again, have we asked why? Do we understand the questions and needs of these young Catholics? Today we speak about evangelization as going to the margins of church and society. Here we have a population that is crucial for the vitality of US Catholicism in this century living in the margins, very likely to lose any connection with the center. Fewer than half of Latinos under age thirty are Catholic (45 percent).[19]

The New Evangelization is far from a ministry of maintenance. It is ultimately a call to mission first and foremost among all the baptized who have lost their zeal.[20] In the words of the bishops of Latin America and the Caribbean, gathered in Aparecida, Brazil, in 2007, it is a call to "missionary discipleship."[21] It is imperative that we develop models of preaching, faith formation, and evangelization that challenge Latino Catholics who are drifting away. We must preach Christ anew, yet in a language that young Latinos in the United States can relate to. There is no doubt that many of the questions of these young women and men will find some resonance in the richness of the Scriptures and the tradition, but we need to listen to their questions and understand them in light of the context within which these are being formulated. Waiting in our rectories or offices for them to come to us might not be the best approach. We must go where they are.

Toward a New Pentecost

The evangelization of Latino Catholics is a unique opportunity for the church in the United States to experience a New Pentecost.[22] The Latino presence is a blessing expressed in the vitality and youth of its people, the diversity of perspectives that encompass the Latino spectrum of cultural experiences, the richness of the cultural and religious traditions that carry the essence of Catholicism from generation to generation, the strong sense of family and community that characterize the Latino worldview, the challenges that many Latinos face, and the desire of many to assume protagonism in the church at a point in history when the church is called to a New Evangelization.[23]

The more we understand the complexity of the questions and realities of Latino Catholics, the more effective we will be as evangelizers in building communities of faith where Latinos, particularly Latino youth, find themselves at home. In the previous section of this chapter we identified three main groups of Latino Catholics along with a number of challenges that each faces in the process of discerning their Catholic identity in this country. As we have said repeatedly, much of the future of Catholicism in the United States depends on how we walk with Latinos, empower them, and encourage them to take the Catholic experience to the next level in the history of the country. The demographics are clear. So are the challenges that this community faces, which need to be addressed by the whole church, not just Latinos.

Preaching the Good News to Latinos in the context of the New Evangelization in the United States cannot be business as usual. The particularity and the complexity of the Latino experience entail the fostering of a new category of pastoral leaders, religious educators, preachers, and evangelizers who have the appropriate intercultural competencies to work with this important population. As long as there are Spanish-speaking immigrants in our parishes, there will be need for comprehensive ministries in Spanish. Today a full quarter of Catholic parishes serve Latinos in Spanish. It is likely that the number of these communities will increase in years to come. As the number of US-born Catholics grows, so will be the demands of doing ministry in English, yet with what I call "Latino flavor" (*sabor Latino*). This means that preachers and evangelizers must learn the cultural symbols, questions, rituals, and grammar that give meaning to the lives of millions of Latino Catholics in our communities.

Evangelizing Latinos in the twenty-first century also demands new approaches to ministry. More than half of Latinos are not actively involved in the church. Many still hold on to the Catholic values learned in their families but run the risk of drifting away unless we reach out to them with the power of the Good News. In the words of St. Paul, "And how can they hear without someone to preach?" (Rom 10:14). We need preachers and evangelizers that come out of our comfort zones and discard ministerial paradigms that do not respond to the needs of Catholics—Latinos and non-Latinos—in this historical moment. We need to go out with a missionary spirit rather than waiting for Latinos to come to us: go to the fields, factories, neighborhoods. We need to learn the new languages and grammars that Latinos speak (e.g., technology, Spanglish, art). We need to take the initiative to ask Latinos about their passions, concerns, and hopes. Good preaching, good catechesis, good evangelization will integrate what we learn in our conversation with these women and men.

The Latino presence is in many ways an opportunity for the church in the United States to reencounter the beauty of the Gospel and its passion for evangelization. The spiritual thirst among Latinos should encourage preachers and educators to present with creativity the message of the living God who walks with us in history. The social and political struggles that Latinos face in their everyday experience should encourage us to revisit the best of Catholic social teaching. The increasing need for pastoral leaders should be an invitation to mentor Latinos at all levels to assume their protagonist role in this historical moment. The sense of *fiesta* and communality characteristic of many Latino cultures should be integrated into life-giving worship.

That is what a New Pentecost is about: allowing the Holy Spirit to guide us in a new time in our shared history. Much has changed in the church in the United States in the last few decades and much will continue to change. This is the right time for Latinos and all other Catholics walking with them to be protagonists of the New Evangelization. This is the right time to write the next chapter in the history of US Catholicism, a chapter that will tell future generations how we facilitated the encounter of Latinos and many others with the person of Jesus Christ here and now.

Endnotes

1. See US Conference of Catholic Bishops, "Hispanic Ministry at a Glance," http://www.usccb.org/issues-and-action/cultural-diversity/hispanic-latino/demographics/hispanic-ministry-at-a-glance.cfm.

2. See Mark M. Gray, Mary L. Gautier, and Melissa A. Cidade, *The Changing Face of U.S. Catholic Parishes*, Emerging Models of Pastoral Leadership (Washington, DC: CARA, 2011), http://cara.georgetown.edu/CARAServices/Parishes%20Phase%20One.pdf.

3. This is the spirit of St. John Paul II's message when he first articulated what the New Evangelization was to be: "The commemoration of the half millennium of evangelization will gain its full energy if it is a commitment, not to re-evangelize but to a New Evangelization, new in its ardor, methods and expression" (John Paul II, Address to CELAM [Opening Address of the Sixth General Assembly of CELAM, 9 March 1983, Port-au-Prince, Haiti], *L'Osservatore Romano*, English ed. 16/780 [18 April 1983]: 9).

4. I have written several essays on US Latino Catholics and the New Evangelization. The following four, which are part of a series, seem most relevant to complement the present reflection. Hosffman Ospino, "Engaging Hispanic Youth," *Pastoral Liturgy* 45, no. 5 (September/October 2014): 9–13; "The U.S. Hispanic Catholic Experience and the New Evangelization: Considerations," *Pastoral Liturgy* 44, no. 4 (September/October 2013): 9–15; "Wisdom from the Church in Latin America on the New Evangelization," *Pastoral Liturgy* 44, no. 3 (July/August 2013): 4–10; "The New Evangelization in a Culturally Diverse Church: Culture Matters," *Pastoral Liturgy* 44, no. 3 (May/June 2013): 4–9.

5. Hosffman Ospino, *Hispanic Ministry in Catholic Parishes* (Huntington, IN: Our Sunday Visitor, 2015).

6. *Posadas*: Advent Novena commemorating Mary and Joseph's journey to Bethlehem searching for an inn. *Altarcitos*: small altars at home that frequently exhibit religious and personal objects. *Padrinazgos/Padrinos*: godparents; many Latinos consider *padrinos* members of the family. *Quinceañera*: celebration of a young woman's fifteenth birthday, a ritual of transition into a more responsible life and preparation for adulthood.

7. For instance, the feast of Our Lady of Guadalupe (common among Mexicans, Mexican Americans, and Central Americans), or the feast of El Señor de los Milagros (common among Peruvians), or the feast of the Santo Niño de Atocha (common among Guatemalans).

8. See Ospino, *Hispanic Ministry in Catholic Parishes*, 10. In the 1980s, only 15 percent of Catholic parishes had developed some form of Hispanic ministry.

9. See ibid., 42.

10. Ibid.

11. See ibid., 19.

12. See ibid., 6.

13. See Cary Funk and Jessica Hamar Martinez, *The Shifting Religious Identity of Latinos in the United States* (Pew Research Center, 2014), 11, http://www.pewforum.org/files/2014/05/Latinos-and-Religion-05-06-full-report-final.pdf.

14. See Ospino, *Hispanic Ministry in Catholic Parishes*, 9.

15. See Thomas Aquinas, *Summa Theologiae*, Ia, q. 75, a. 5.

16. See the following works exploring more in depth the complexity of the youth ministry among Latino Catholics in the United States: Ken Johnson-Mondragón, "Hispanic Youth and Young Adult Ministry," in *Hispanic Ministry in the 21st Century: Present and Future*, ed. Hosffman Ospino (Miami, FL: Convivium, 2010); National Catholic Network de Pastoral Juvenil Hispana (La Red), *Conclusions: First National Encounter for Hispanic Youth and Young Adult Ministry* (Washington, DC: United States Conference of Catholic Bishops, 2008); Johnson-Mondragón, ed., *Pathways of Hope and Faith Among Hispanic Teens: Pastoral Reflections and Strategies Inspired by the National Study of Youth and Religion* (Stockton, CA: Instituto Fe y Vida, 2007).

17. See Funk and Hamar Martinez, *The Shifting Religious Identity of Latinos*, 5, 14.

18. See ibid., 9, 12–13.

19. See ibid., 10.

20. "The new evangelization, then, which is primarily a task-to-be-done and a spiritual challenge, is the responsibility of all Christians who are in serious pursuit of holiness. In this context and with this understanding of formation, it will be useful to dedicate space and time to considering the institutions and means available to local Churches to make baptized persons more conscious of their duty in missionary work and evangelization" (Synod of Bishops, XIII Ordinary General Assembly, The New Evangelization for the Transmission of the Christian Faith: *Lineamenta* [2011], 22).

21. See Fifth General Conference of Latin American and Caribbean Bishops in Aparecida, Brazil (2007), Conclusions 156, 172, http://www.celam.org/conferencia_aparecida.php.

22. I use the expression "a New Pentecost" in line with the Conclusions of Aparecida. The document calls for a change of attitude, a new openness, a new culture of

encounter guided by the Holy Spirit. While it is an invocation asking for the Spirit, such invocation is far from passive. It is a predisposition to be sent as missionary disciples. See Aparecida, Conclusions 548.

23. US Conference of Catholic Bishops, "The Hispanic Presence: Challenge and Commitment" (1983), in *Hispanic Ministry: Three Major Documents* (Washington, DC: USCCB, 1995), 5; National Conference of Catholic Bishops, *The Hispanic Presence in the New Evangelization in the United States* (Washington, DC: USCCB, 1996), 25.

Chapter 10

Ten Ways to Make It Stick:
The Importance of Connection
to Preaching and Teaching

Karla J. Bellinger

We live in a distracted and overcommunicated world. Words and words and more words bombard us constantly. One strain of noise yells, "This is important!" A second set of voices shouts, "You need to hear this!" A third simply points a finger and screeches, "You should!" What is it we should hear, and what is so important? "Buy this!" "Do this!" "Believe this!" "Share (or tweet) this!" "Come to this!" "Join this!" A constant "you should" pervades our world. When all of those voices are thrown together, the noise grows louder and louder and louder. And how do the people listening respond? They yell, "Aaahhh!!" and tune it out.

What we have to say, the Gospel that we preach, is it just one more thing in the midst of so much clatter and chatter and confusion? The world is so full of messages—how do we get *our* message out there? How can we be memorable people and pass on a memorable message in a world that has a hard time remembering anything? What are concrete ways to be more effective and better connect with the people we serve? That is the focus of this workshop.

The Role of Memory

Memory is important to advertisers. They would like us to remember their slogans so that we will buy their products. See if you can put the correct brand name into the blanks: The "_____" bunny just keeps going and going and going; "_____": Just do it; "_____": Melts in your mouth, not in your hand. How readily a thought comes to mind is called salience: these little ditties readily pop into our minds so that we remember them.

Memory also has a more profound role in our lives. That deeper place of memory is the space out of which we operate. Imagine a beautiful picture of a field with a blue sky and fluffy white clouds. In the foreground of the image is a deeply shaded thicket. Now visualize a baby deer hiding in that dark thicket. From out of that hidden space, he can see the bright sunshine and the white clouds passing by, but secluded in his hidden space, he is out of sight. Similarly, inside each of us is a hidden and sheltered place of memory.

Take a moment and close your eyes. Go down into that place of memory and look at what is there—think back to your youngest moment. What is deeply within you? Some of you may encounter joyful memories. Some of those recollections may be painful ones—like a baby fawn who has to lie among prickles and thorns, you may not want to lie down there. Your earliest memories may recall a mother deer comforting you; or you could be like Bambi and the mother deer is gone and the memory that arises is a lonely one. Whatever is there, it is deep inside of yourself, known to you alone. Come out of that memory without losing the sense of it and open your eyes: as you look at the lights, the people, the clouds, you see that the outside world in which you function is bright and busy. Nobody knows that deep place of memory inside of you. It is yours alone.

Those of us who preach and who teach and who minister seek to communicate from those deep places within us to the deepest places within our people—that is what we mean when we say that we want to "connect." That is what *they* mean when *they* ask us to "connect" or to "relate to them." We can throw out superficial formulae, like "Things go better with Coke" and "Jesus died because he loves us." We can stay on that level. But to deeply impact people's lives, we have to work from our memory, from our deep place and touch them in their deep places. How do we do that? And why does it matter?

Memory in Christian Tradition

When we look at Christian tradition, memory is at its core. "Don't forget your people, O God!" cry the Israelites in the desert. "Remember that you were slaves in Egypt and the Lord redeemed you," pleads

Jeremiah. "Even if a mother forgets her child, I will not forget you," proclaims Isaiah. "Lift up your hand, O God. Will you forget me forever?" laments the psalmist. Jesus says, "Do this in remembrance of me." Saint Dismas calls out from the cross, "Jesus, remember me, when you come into your kingdom."

One of the deepest hungers in human existence is to be remembered: to be wanted, to be recognized, to be known, to be kept in the mind of another. And to be forgotten—and this is the peril of refugees in camps, the people who drown on boats trying to escape to freedom, and the children abandoned and turned back at our borders—is one of the deepest hurts of human life. Those who are lost or forgotten or abandoned are not just in the big "issues." The distraught and lonely and forlorn are also sitting in our pews on Sunday.

Bringing People into an Encounter with God

Stop a moment and think of a time when God remembered you, a time when you were most connected with God. Bring that experience up from your deep recesses of memory and take a look at it. Where have you encountered God in your life? What do you remember?

This word "encounter" has grown in importance in Catholic writings. Why? To encounter God is the beginning of relationship. It is through the Holy Spirit's initiative that we encounter God. The US Catholic bishops' new document speaks of bringing people into an encounter with God through preaching. Benedict talked of encounter. Pope Francis talks of encounter.

What are we seeking in preaching? The homily is not just a seven-to-ten-minute string of words sitting in the middle of a liturgy. The homily is integral to the liturgy. The purpose of liturgy is to bring people into an encounter with God; therefore, the goal of Sunday preaching is to also further that purpose. That sets the bar for the homily really high. What is the ideal? We seek to facilitate an encounter with the living God. When you are done preaching, your goal is not for people to say, "Wow! Father (Deacon or Bishop) ___ is a good guy and a great preacher!" but rather, "Wow! God is good!"

A memorable person plus a memorable message can be a powerful influence on a person's life. Think about somebody who has been memorable in your life; one who impacted you, one who influenced you. What made that person memorable?

How can *we*, similarly, be memorable people? How can *we* impact other people?

Ten Ways to Make It Stick

The seeds of this workshop were planted in an earlier workshop that I did at the National Catholic Educational Association convention titled "10 Ways to Make Human Connection with Today's Catholic Youth." Where did I get that input on connection? I surveyed 561 Catholic high school students for my doctoral study titled, "Are You Talking to Me? A Study of Young Listeners' Connection with Catholic Sunday Preaching." I asked the kids, "Who connects with you? How do those 'connectors' connect? What would you tell the preachers in your parish about how to connect with you better?" Their responses helped to inform my book *Connecting Pulpit and Pew: Breaking Open the Conversation about Catholic Preaching*.[1] One of those ten ways of connecting, the role of memory, has consistently resonated deeply, and from that felt need, this workshop that delves into the principles of "stickiness" was born.

Memory → *Belief* → *Attitude* → *Behavior*

One of the fundamental progressions in the study of memory is that memory fuels belief; belief impacts attitude; and attitude drives behavior. We often want to start at the end of the progression: we want people to change their behavior; we want them to do something different because of what we have preached to them. But if they don't alter their attitude to change their behavior, they are not going to act differently. And if their belief has not changed, then their attitude is not going to change. Thus memory is at the source of behavior.

Let me give you an example. You and your brother go to a family reunion. Great-aunt Priscilla walks into the room. Great-aunt Priscilla is somebody that you absolutely adore—you remember sitting down and reading with her when you were five years old; you recall the gentleness of her hands, the tenderness of her voice, and the smell of her perfume . . . You have a brother, on the other hand, who mutters, "Oh, my God, here comes Great-aunt Priscilla!" and he hides in the bathroom. He remembers when she smacked him on the hand with a ruler. Why do the two of you behave differently toward Great-aunt Priscilla? Your behavior comes out of your dissimilar attitudes toward her. Those attitudes came out of the beliefs that you (and he) have about her, which are built on your individual memories of Great-aunt Priscilla. Your memories may or may not have anything to do with the ninety-three-year-old lady who just walked into the room.

Let me give you another example. When I trained youth ministers for the Diocese of Cleveland, I routinely asked the participants in the ecclesiology workshop, "What is your earliest memory of church?" One woman who had been in youth ministry for forty years said, "I remember sitting on my grandma's lap. Being in church when I was about four years old was the safest place to be. I have worked in the church in some way ever since." Others spoke of candles, or priests and/or sisters, or May crowning, or family events. Their earliest memories of "church" were very warm and very positive. For you who work in the church, at some point you are likely to have had some very positive memory of being affiliated with this institution or you would not have given it your life. That memory drives your belief, which then impacts your attitude, which then affects your behavior.

How does this matter to preaching? You create memories when you preach. (You hope those memories will be good ones.) You can spend eight hours on your homily, but if you do not pay attention to how it is connecting with the memory of the listener, that is time wasted. I haven't yet met a person in ministry who has time to waste.

Is this process set in stone? No: it can work the other way around also. A change in behavior can also create a different story. Let's say a thirteen-year-old comes from a highly moral family. He goes to summer camp and all the boys in his cabin are looking at *Playboy* magazine. He doesn't really want to look at *Playboy* magazine, but as the week goes on, he starts to sneak a peek at the girly pictures and he starts to like them. After he gets home, he starts to regularly look at pornography online. Thus his behavior has changed. At first, that behavioral change will be uncomfortable for him. Then he begins to change his attitude: "Well, that's not so bad. . . . " So he changes his belief about pornography ("My parents are just stuck in the dark ages"), and thus he recasts the memory of his experience. What used to be uncomfortable is not difficult any longer. He is creating a different memory by changing his mental story.

This reversal often happens when kids go to college. Their memories of church and their beliefs and attitudes may be positive when they leave high school. When they get to college, they may begin to engage in behaviors that at first make them uncomfortable. To get rid of the discomfort, they change their attitude, their beliefs, and ultimately, they recast how they tell the story inside their heads.

Principle One: We Operate from Our Internal Story

The first principle of "making it stick"[2] is that we each operate out of these internal stories. Some preachers feel that they are preaching into a vacuum on Sunday morning. Nothing could be farther from the truth. More than a thousand stories slide into your pews. If you connect with those mental stories, your people will relate to your message. If you ignore those internal stories and do not connect with them, the TV set inside their brains will continue to flash their own images, and your words will be tuned out and not be heard.

How do we recast stories? Think of the pictures of the smiling Pope Francis. This man has recast the story of "Catholic Church." People of all faiths and persuasions are starting to see the church differently because of him. He is not giving us new doctrine. He is not changing Catholic practice (as much as the media would like us to think so). What is he doing? He is telling the story in a different way. The memory of "Catholic Church" has grown more positive, even if much on the ground hasn't changed. The belief about the church has shifted, and thus attitudes have also shifted. It may be too early to measure the "Francis Effect" on behavior, but memories, beliefs, and attitudes have definitely altered. We are operating out of a new story.

Christian Smith speaks of the story that young people tell themselves about God: God is useful; he is like a butler who comes at our convenience when we call him; he wants us to be nice; and good people go to heaven. This is what Smith defines as Moralistic Therapeutic Deism;[3] it is not Christianity. This story of God is not just in the minds of our youth; it is also the predominant story of most post–Vatican II parents. Therefore in our preaching, we have to recognize the story that is running in our listeners' heads and speak to it. We may have to retell the story about God in that context and recast the story of Christianity so that those who are "almost Christian" can grasp the meaning of sacrifice and salvation.

If we are working with four-year-olds, we are not recasting a story. We are creating a story: about God, about Jesus, about church, about parish community, and about family. Early memories are highly formative. Children will operate out of that deep space of memory as adults.

Principle Two: Negative Memories Weigh Heavily

How often have you been complimented on your preaching or your speaking? How often have you been criticized? Which one comes more readily to your mind? Negative memories weigh heavily.

I recall doing a workshop at a catechetical conference in 1998. It was a very interactive workshop and the catechists were loving it until I had them do Jesus Jacks (a variation of jumping jacks) with a shout of "J-E-S-U-S, Go, Jesus!" One elderly woman in the back wrote on my evaluation, "She's not my style." How many positive evaluations did I get and how many others have I gotten in all of the intervening years, and which comment do you think that I still remember?

Perhaps you have heard some variation of this comment: "Do you remember when Father 'so-and-so,' twenty-five years ago, said 'such and such' to Great-aunt Mabel's cousin's nephew? And that's why we don't go to church." That's a negative family memory. Negative memories weigh heavily. Advertisers say that if you get negative buzz, it takes twelve positive experiences to outweigh that one negative. I would say, with the authority and the credibility and the high expectations for the church and the clergy, that twelve to one is nowhere near the right number: a hundred to one, maybe; a thousand to one, more likely. One extremely negative comment about you, about your ministry, about your parish . . . it can make a big impact. If someone you really care about says something unexpectedly critical, you may not be able to get that out of your head and it may infect that relationship. Negative memories weigh really heavily.

What difference does this make for preaching? All preachers should take the medical doctor's Hippocratic oath: "First, do no harm." Especially at sensitive times—like funerals, Christmas, Easter, and with someone whom you have never seen before—your words may form their entire impression of the Catholic Church. Don't do anything to hurt or slight or be dismissive or disrespectful. Your two words or even the quality of your handshake or your smile may form that person's entire impression of the Catholic Church. Is it fair? No. Is it real? Yes.

Principle Three: The Unexpected (Disconfirmation) Is Memorable

One of the consistent comments about Catholic preaching in my study of young people was, "It's the same old, same old." The kids said, "Monotony kills interest" and "Sing a new song for once." The people in the pews tune out when they get the same message over and over again.

On the other hand, the unexpected is totally memorable. The term "disconfirmed expectancy" means that whatever expectation that is running in your listeners' heads is contradicted by what they see. As a result, they grow a little uncomfortable and/or curious and start to pay closer attention. So whatever your people are expecting, turn it upside down.

First a caution: I have heard the story of a priest who walked up to the pulpit with an umbrella while blasting out the song "Singing in the Rain." His whole parish remembers it. I have asked several parishioners, "What was the point of the homily?" Every one of them has told me, "I don't know. I don't remember." It *was* memorable. But that memory didn't help them to encounter God. Unexpected shouldn't just serve itself. Unexpected is sticky because it disconfirms expectations and helps people to internalize the message. "Lowry's Loop"[4] uses this technique in the way it structures a homily—unsettle, then turn the story on its head, and recast the expectation toward the Gospel. The Gospel is the goal.

Let me give you an example where this was done well. One young man in my study wrote about when he went to a conference. A bishop gave a homily about when he had doubts about God as a teenager. This kid was totally taken aback by that, and thus he remembered the entire homily. His conclusion was, "It is okay if I have doubts, because they will work out. After all, he's a bishop and he had doubts." What teenager is expecting a bishop to have doubts about faith? As a result, the homilist was more persuasive because he disconfirmed the youth's expectation. From laypeople's point of view, clergy are supposed to be perfect, or at least nearly perfect. There's a pedestal effect in both preaching and teaching, so don't air your dirty laundry, but from time to time, give your people something that is a little unexpected or out of the ordinary. Get them out of their comfort zone and keep them on their toes. Carefully.

You can also do this in a simple way when unpacking a text. Tell the story from the point of view of an unexpected character. I once crafted a reflection for young women from the point of view of a young woman who was not allowed in the synagogue. She sat outside. The men came storming out of the synagogue shouting, "Who does he think he is—the bread of life! Bah! We will no longer walk with him!" She told that story to her grandchildren as a "back-in-the-day" story and (in my imagination) one of them wrote it down. So be creative. Don't fall into the rut of the same kind of homily every week. Keep growing and learning and trying new things.

There is something unexpected going on right now that has captured our attention: Pope Francis keeps doing things like driving a subcompact car, eating in the cafeteria with the housekeeping and janitorial staffs, letting little boys sit in the papal chair, and telling us that he is a sinner. These are not actions that we "expect" from a pope. He keeps surprising us, in a good way. As a result, his actions are "sticky" and he himself is memorable.

Principle Four: Be Concrete. Does This Pertain to Me?

In my study, when I asked how to connect with them in the homily, Catholic high school students repeatedly said, "Relate to me." As they are listening to you, they mentally ask, "Is this related to my life?" "Does this matter?" If your homily preaches about how much we love our grandchildren, who are you talking to? Grandparents. Who are you not talking to? Grandchildren. Yet they may be sitting together in the same pew. You just marginalized one of them as though they were not there.

When you get home from a conference or a vacation, you may have a desk full of mail or an inbox full of email. As you sort through that huge stack, what do you implicitly ask yourself? "Does this pertain to me?" If no, then into the trash . . . delete . . . it goes. As you sort: "Oh, here's a bill! I'd better save that." "Wow! A letter!" This is our way of thinking. In our overcommunicated world, it's like we have shrunk the intake valve and we won't let things in if they don't pertain to us. There is just too much noise saying, "This is important." "Listen to me!" "You should." It has to pertain to us or we shut it out. "Oh, you are talking to grandparents, that must not pertain to me," thinks the teenager, so she starts to think about going to work at Starbucks after Mass and what she needs to do to get ready. It is just like sorting through the mail: Does this pertain to me?

Homilists wonder, how can you talk to a seven-year-old, a forty-seven-year-old, and an eighty-seven-year-old at the same time? One way is to be concrete, especially in the naming of emotions. Can you find a concrete emotion in the story? For example, in the story that I mentioned earlier, people departed when Jesus said, "I am the Bread of Life." What happens when someone leaves us? Almost every person in the pew knows what it feels like for someone to leave them. What does it feel like? What does it taste like to lose somebody or have somebody go away? I asked my five-year-old granddaughter, "What has been the saddest time in your life?" She said, "When my mommy went away for the night when

I was three." Just about everybody, from three to eighty-nine to a hundred and five, has had the experience of people going away. The emotion ties us together. A seven-year-old remembers what it is like to go to kindergarten all by himself. An eighty-seven-year-old knows what it feels like to lose her husband. A forty-year-old knows what it is like to lose his mother or son. If we seek to connect and build memories, we speak to our people's deep memories in a concrete way. When have you yourself had that experience? What did it feel like for you? You may not end up telling your story. But tell your story to yourself. As a result, by your words and by your tone, your people will know that you have been there too.

To be concrete, have something in it for those who taste, for those who hear, those who touch, who feel, who see. Can you smell it? Can you see it, hear it, feel it, taste it? As I listen to speakers and preachers, there is much abstraction. We use churchy words without being concrete about them. What does grace smell like? What does salvation feel like? What does redemption look like? Can we be concrete? Can we name it in a way that people have experienced it? If we don't, we're just going over their heads, and again, we're just wasting our time and theirs. Our words and images that we use have to resonate with our people's concrete experience.

Principle Five: One Simple Big Idea? What Path Can You Take to Get There Memorably?

When you've only got seven to ten minutes, you have to have one simple big idea, one overarching idea. If you have one point and one focus, how then do you flesh out that theme to touch your people?

There are pathways through which people encounter God. Pope Francis, in *Evangelii Gaudium*, puts it well: within your one central idea, have a thought (for the left brain), an image (for the right-brain people), and a sentiment (for people who process through the heart). To remember it, think of it as the SIT formula—sentiment, image, thought. What clergy have shared with me is that much of seminary education trains you along the left brain, the thought pathway. When you are beginning to preach, you may assume that the people in the pew are thinking along with you. That may or may not be true. Right-brained people process through images in their minds. Also the less someone is invested in your message, the more that the message will come to them peripherally through impressions. They may not have the vocabulary to process it; they may have back pain and thus be unable to focus; they may not have the mental ability to think it through; they may be young and have no experience or understanding of what you are saying.

Those who form impressions evaluate: What's his tone of voice? Is "Father" friendly? "I don't get what he is saying," but the impression that "he's a nice guy" may be the beginning of their attention. Images like "smell like sheep" also capture attention. Other people are heart-related; if you share an emotion with them, they will feel it.

You focus on one idea, but there are pathways to take you there. You may have one message, but you are looking for three things: (1) "I get it!" (2) "I feel it!" and (3) "I see it!" With thought, when you mentally embrace something, you think, "I get it!" (the pathway of thought). With image, it's a different way of "getting it." You see a mental picture—"I see it!" (the pathway of image). When it touches the heart, the listener responds, "I feel it!" (emotion/sentiment). When someone walks away from your preaching and says, "I don't get anything out of it," it means that the mode of the message that you are sending is not the pathway through which they receive. So broaden out the main point of your preaching to make sure that you include a sentiment, image, and thought (SIT).

Principle Six: To Motivate, Tie In and S-T-R-E-T-C-H

Imagine a picture of the top of Mont Blanc. Skiers take the cable car all the way to the top of the mountain and then walk along a steep ridge to ski down into a pristine white "bowl." Why do they do that? It is exhilarating; it gets the heart pumping and the adrenaline rushing; it is highly motivating. Is the joy of Jesus that exhilarating for us? Are we as motivated toward preaching the Gospel as those who ski at the top of the world?

What motivates people? I once asked a professor who was skilled in consumer behavior, "What do you do about unmotivated people?" He said, "There are no unmotivated people." Let me put that down in capital letters: THERE ARE NO UNMOTIVATED PEOPLE. Why? *Something* gets everybody out of bed in the morning. *Something.* Duty, love, fear, or the smell of coffee: *something* motivates each person. The question isn't "Are they motivated?" or "Are they unmotivated?" The question is "What drives them?" A dad may wonder, "Why can't I get 'the kid' to (fill in the blank) and do what I want him to do?" The "kid" may not be motivated toward what his dad wants. For someone far from faith, the Eucharist just doesn't matter all that much; her Sunday morning running group may matter to her more.

In order to motivate, then, first find out what the other person values. I listened to a (very Catholic) grandmother as we stood around a campfire. She told me about her fourteen-year-old grandson who had just gone to "motocross weekend" at the hilly state park south of us. Motocross weekend was only for high school boys, sponsored by a "big box" church nearby. Her grandson was thrilled about the experience. All day they had roared their bikes up and down the trails. In the evening, they had sat around the campfire and the youth minister talked to them about Jesus. The kid came back from the weekend motivated to follow Jesus . . . at that church down the road. What was the key? The youth program knew how to tie into what that lad valued, which made him receptive to their message.

In preaching, we tie in and then we stretch. What do your people value? What is deepest in their hearts? Parents may value that their kids have faith. They may value that their children get good grades and grow up to be responsible. These are their values. Tie into those values, but don't stay at "be nice." That's not enough. Stretch them to the Gospel. Tie and then stretch.

For fifty years, we have argued: Do we tie into the culture or do we preach the time-tested Gospel? Two camps in the church have warred with each other since the Second Vatican Council. I was raised as a Presbyterian, so I come to the church with an outsider perspective: What are we fighting about? We either tie in *or* we stretch? No. We tie in *and* we stretch. We have to do both.

We have a rich tradition to stretch people toward. As I worked on my master's degree in systematic theology at Notre Dame, I fell in love with Catholic theology. We have a rich tradition, deeper than any of us can ever grasp. But we have to tie that into daily life—we are not selling out by connecting to life because we will not be content to leave people there. We then stretch them to the Gospel: to give them words of hope in times of despair, to offer a taste of trust when life feels uncertain, to show them One who is strength when they feel weak. We preach the paschal mystery. To motivate, we tie in with what they hold dear, and then we stretch.

Principle Seven: Be Credible

My grandfather was an avid St. Louis Cardinals fan. At the seventh inning, everybody stands up. Try this exercise sometime. Find one other person.

The question here is, "Who is credible in our culture?" One of you be a teenager; the other is an adult. For one whole minute, you the adult, tell the teenager what he or she should do. You the teenager, you only have two words to say: "Who says?" Go. After one minute, switch sides.

How did that feel? Some typical responses I get to this exercise: "Frustrating!" "You don't know how to respond to it!" "If there is no punishment, telling them what to do is going to go nowhere—with no consequences. . . . " "I grew up in a household where you didn't say 'who says!'; you would have gotten a smack." "If you really cared about the adult, you might not keep saying 'who says?'" "I literally could not form a sentence telling someone what to do, my mind does not think in action-based morality—it was very difficult." For those of you who were teenagers, how did that feel? "I loved it!" "Empowering, wasn't it?" "Ooh!" (exhilaration)!

We have a culture that asks, "Who says?" A crisis of authority has been building for several decades. How can you be credible as a homilist? How can you have people listen to you? "Who says" that the church is right?

Before the advent of the printing press in the late fifteenth century, the source of authority was the community. Church leadership carried much weight, and the people listened to them. With the advent of the printing press, sources of authority shifted—the "book" became the authority. "The Bible says" became the rallying cry of the Reformation. Even now, if you are in the academic world, if you're widely published, you are an authority. We are now in a third wave. When I asked my sixteen-year-old daughter about sources of authority for her generation, she said, "I can always find another spin on the internet." Thus, the prevailing attitude has become, "Who says you're right?"

At the same time (and this is good news for people who work in ministry), sources of influence are still close to home. Parents and family members and friends are still consistently rated as the greatest sources of influence. In a world that seems so disconnected, that opens an incredible opportunity for a credible and caring preacher, teacher, or minister. If you can make those connections, you actually have a greater opportunity to make an impact than you did thirty years ago when people trusted the media. You may have to earn that authority. You may have to take the time to connect. You may have to listen in order to know what matters to your people, but the opportunity is there. They will listen if you connect with their deepest needs.

Principle Eight: Tell the Story of Beauty

We have a countercultural message. The God we serve is Beauty. To follow our God takes heroism, goodness, sacrifice, noble adventure, fervor, commitment, loyalty, solidarity, and hope. What other cause is so worthy? Augustine captured it when he said, "Late have I loved You, O Beauty ever ancient, ever new . . ."[5] There is not a lot of beauty explicit in our world. We seem to be surrounded by the bad news of war and murder, disease and destruction. We have to tell a different story.

One of the roles of a preacher is to name the beauty of God. That begins, of course, by *seeing* the grandeur of God. We come to that understanding through prayer, through Scripture, through nature, through music, through liturgy, through good food, and through our interactions with people. The experience of beauty is worth cultivating, worth taking the time for us to experience so that we can share it.

The story of beauty is the noble adventure of the Gospel: the person of Jesus given to redeem us, to lift us up, to inspire us. The message that we have to pass on is the most beautiful of all. John Paul II was particularly good at this principle of stickiness. He inspired young people when he said, "Remember: Christ is calling you; the Church needs you; the Pope believes in you and he expects great things of you!"[6] Following his example, stretch your people a little bit to be more noble, to be a little more courageous. If you stretch too far, the message snaps and then seems unattainable. You stretch too little and no one grows. Preach something beautiful for God.

I was sitting in church a couple of weeks ago and right in front of me was a boy and his father. The boy was about nine. I couldn't figure out what was the matter with his hair. When he stood up, I saw that he had a bolt recently inserted into his skull and the hair had not yet grown back. What was going through the boy's mind? What was going through his father's mind? The message from the pulpit was "be nice" and "work a little harder this week." How did that message give hope to this man and his son? Two rows ahead of me was a friend whom I knew about ten years ago when our kids were in classes together. One of her sons committed suicide three weeks ago. I don't know that she can work harder this week. She is just barely coping as it is.

Finally, believe in the beauty of your people. In some parishes there is a large gap between pulpit and pew. This is unfortunate. As the spiritual leader, your attitude toward your people leaks into your preaching.

If you don't like them, they will pick that up. If you believe in them, love them, and call them to be their best selves, they will rise to that expectation. We are all to embrace the call to holiness, none excluded, and nothing less: pass on the call of Beauty.

Principle Nine: Be There—Use Focused Attention, Two-Minute Eye Contact, Be a One-Minute Listener

How can you be a memorable person? Everybody is busy. You may be busy as a priest or a deacon or bishop. The people in the pews are also busy and harried and stressed. Studies have shown that at least 30 to 40 percent of working people and students feel that they are overworked. (Actually, that is something that you could preach on: "I feel overwhelmed, how about you? What might Jesus have to say about that? Do you think Jesus ever felt overwhelmed?")

How can you be a memorable person? Be there. Even when you are busy, be there for people. The person that you found memorable in our discussion earlier—when you needed them, were they there for you? Did they give you focused attention? Did they give you loving eye contact? Did they listen to you? We can take that memorable person as a model for how we can also "be there" for others.

Specific skills help us to connect. Try two seconds of eye contact: put all the love you can into your eyes and look at someone for two seconds. Give it a try. Not ten seconds or they will feel intimidated. I have been a soccer coach and a volleyball coach, and yes, if you want to intimidate a difficult player, you give him a good long stare. But, no, two seconds of loving eye contact shows them you care.

A second skill is to be a one-minute listener. Listen in a focused way without being distracted. It is actually very hard in our culture; we have learned how not to pay attention. As you are listening to another, how often are you thinking, "I wonder what my email is doing . . . ?" Something goes buzz and suddenly we are no longer listening. Try focused listening for one whole minute. An effective preacher is first and foremost a good listener.

When I recently gave this workshop, the spiritual director of a seminary asked me, "Could you teach our seminarians this?" These two simple things: two seconds of loving eye contact and one minute of focused listening can make a difference. Both pass the message that the other person matters, that you are "there" for them, and that you can be trusted. Think of its opposite—with no eye contact and dismissive listening, you communicate the message that they don't matter to you. Even if you feel kindness about them emotionally, your love is not effectively communicated *to* them. (Note that these mannerisms are culturally conditioned: different cultures "pass" love in various ways; find out how caring is communicated in that culture.)

If you are walking past somebody in the street, especially if you are wearing your clerical garb, giving two seconds of loving eye contact can make a powerful impact in their life. Look at our earlier picture of Pope Francis. People think he has a nice smile. But look more closely—it's the love in his eyes that captures you. Do the same.

Principle Ten: Be Passionate about the Gospel

Can you preach out of that deep place of memory, from the inner fire of encounter, if you are burned out and weary and you have nothing left to give? When you are not spiritually healthy and taking care of yourself, that's when you become one of those monotonous people who preach the same old thing every single Sunday. Do you think that your people cannot tell?

You yourself have to keep that deep place of memory intact for you to pass it on. In one of my clergy interviews, one priest said, "I think that we need a renewal." Preaching is a spiritual discipline: to ponder and pray over the Scriptures, to be attuned to the needs of your people, to craft images, thoughts, and sentiments that resonate with your people—that is demanding work! To preach effectively requires much energy.

An older priest told me, "You know, it used to be when I was young that I could say to the secretary, 'Tell everyone to go away, I am taking a nap.' Imagine that nowadays!" In coaching preaching, I have noticed that the most resonant homilies are the ones that follow right after a retreat.

You are an icon, a window into God. You cannot get out of the way—when you preach, you are the way. Be passionate about what you are preaching; allow yourself to fall deeply in love with Jesus. Like Jeremiah's fire in the bones, let the Good News burn within you so brightly that you cannot hold it in! None of us is ever done growing in one's abilities to embody this message, to be a memorable person passing on a memorable message. A consistent request from the young people in my study was, "Go deeper." The psalmist also says, "Deep calls to deep" (Ps 42:8). Let us not be afraid to go deeper into those places where God dwells.

Conclusion

The world is so full of noise. For a message to be memorable, to matter deeply: we tell the story; be concrete; be simple; be unexpected; tie into real life and then stretch; be credible; and show that it matters. That's the message.

To be a credible messenger, be someone who is "there" for others: give focused attention; listen well; use loving eye contact; find things that you have in common; and convey passion. Thus the message and the messenger together will be transformative and life-changing.

For each person we meet, in each moment, be present to them. We never know what we've got until we don't have it; how long we've got until the time is gone. Now is the time. This is the place. If this message was memorable for you, if this message stuck, find somebody else to tell and pass it on. And try one of these principles every month as an experiment and see how it goes. God bless you and your preaching.

Endnotes

1. Karla J. Bellinger, *Connecting Pulpit and Pew: Breaking Open the Conversation about Catholic Preaching* (Collegeville, MN: Liturgical Press, 2014).

2. See Chip Heath and Dan Heath, *Made to Stick: Why Some Ideas Survive and Others Die* (New York: Random House, 2008).

3. Christian Smith, "Is Moralistic Therapeutic Deism the New Religion of American Youth?," in *Passing on the Faith: Transforming Traditions for the Next Generation of Jews, Christians, and Muslims*, ed. James L. Heft, 55–74 (New York: Fordham University Press, 2006).

4. See Eugene L. Lowry, *The Homiletical Plot: The Sermon as Narrative Art Form*, expanded ed. (Louisville: Westminster John Knox, 2001); and Lowry, *The Sermon: Dancing the Edge of Mystery* (Nashville: Abingdon Press, 1997).

5. St. Augustine, *Confessions*, bk. 10, 27.

6. Address of John Paul II to the Young People at the Kiel Center, St. Louis, January 26, 1999, http://w2.vatican.va/content/john-paul-ii/en/travels/1999/documents/hf_jp-ii_spe_26011999_stlouis-youth.html.

Chapter 11

Preaching the Language of Yes

Susan McGurgan

In a reflection given the day before the consistory, which created twenty-two new cardinals, Cardinal-designate Timothy Dolan of New York noted that the New Evangelization is a call to share what we believe, not simply what we oppose. "The New Evangelization is accomplished with a smile, not a frown. The *missio ad gentes* is all about a yes to everything decent, good, true, beautiful and noble in the human person. The church is about a yes, not a no!"[1] The New Evangelization, in his vision, is a call for the language of "yes"—a language much easier to master in theory than in practice.

Communications experts estimate that we speak approximately sixteen thousand words a day. That adds up to 112,000 words each week and over five million words every year.[2] Although in most cases, we spend very little time analyzing or reflecting upon these words, a word is like a living organism, capable of growing, changing, spreading, and influencing the world, both directly and indirectly. These words are not equal; they do not all carry the same freight. Karl Rahner contrasts the words of facts and information with "depth words," those primordial and revelatory words that embody a deeper reality.[3] These are words that emerge from the deep pools of spirit and experience and they transcend our ability to describe and define them.

Revelatory and symbolic words are not the only words with a powerful impact. Scientists and psychologists have long noted what they call "a negativity bias" in our outlook.[4] We instinctively pay close attention to negative words, images, and experiences, perhaps an evolutionary remnant of our days as hunters and gatherers, when those who ignored negative information or were not alert to danger simply didn't survive. Today, news is transmitted immediately. A person who is not directly affected by the news event nevertheless experiences it viscerally. We are "alert to danger" via a twenty-four-hour news cycle that reports not only events but our reactions to events and even our reactions to reactions. This affects our language in significant and powerful ways. The shock of 9/11, the church's sexual abuse crisis, Sandy Hook, the Iraq War, hostile political discourse, the economic depression—these events fill our vocabularies with words that both create and sustain the stress they describe: *depression, predator, terrorist, weapons of mass destruction, polarization.* We become numb to euphemisms that mask the true meaning of words: "collateral damage" for the violent wartime deaths of civilians; "outsourcing" as a euphemism for the erosion of jobs and dignity among working men and women; "enhanced interrogation" as a substitute for the words and images of torture.[5]

Our culture encourages us to embrace a bottom-line approach to issues and institutions. What is the quick fix? Who and what solves the problem? This, in turn, promotes a deficit-based or pathology-focused language that speaks to:

> Symptom/clinical diagnosis/treatment protocol
> Systems failure/technical intervention/solution

Without the nuances of divine grace and abiding mercy, this language can lead to a prescriptive or utilitarian view of church. Transferred to the pulpit, our impoverished language contributes to the development of what Pope Francis calls, "Christians whose lives seem like Lent without Easter" (*Evangelii Gaudium* 6).

Language is powerful. As Archbishop Desmond Tutu said, "Language does not just describe reality; language creates the reality it describes."[6] If our words are a verbal hammer, we will look at our people and see a lot that needs pounding. If our language describes Catholic life as a zero-sum game, we will inevitably find winners and losers and deficits that seem impossible to fill. If words are hurled into pews like an IED, we will awaken to a desolate landscape. If the language of preaching is obscure, esoteric, inaccessible, or remote, we will form disciples who believe that God is simply unavailable to them. Proverbs 18:21 reminds us, "Death and life are in the power of the tongue."

Consider totalitarian states in history. One of their first goals is to control language, to crush those buoyant and subversive words that create a space for something new to be born. When Adolf Hitler was appointed chancellor of Germany in 1933, destruction of the free press soon followed. George Orwell's dystopian novel *1984* illustrates the power inherent in the control of language. "By changing the language, it would also change the 'chessboard' of individual thought, determining all its possible 'moves.'"[7]

Gospel preaching, particularly when aimed at evangelization, requires words that are both powerful and free, words that soar and skip and spill over with meaning. These are words that lead us to the brink of what we cannot really say, but understand at some deeper level. Preaching demands language that allows "a deeper mystery, the offer of grace, to become more concretely present and available in human life."[8] These depth words touch and release our deepest fears, hopes, and dreams. The preacher becomes in some ways a "mediator of meaning," who "represents this community by voicing its concerns, by naming its demons and thus enabling it to gain some understanding and control of the evil which afflicts it. He represents the Lord by offering another word, a word of healing and pardon, of acceptance and love."[9] The true power of the preached word lies in its ability to open up new possibilities, to liberate, illuminate, and heal. "Our physical world is polluted with dangerous chemicals, but our language, too, suffers its own kind of pollution. This is an ecological problem that we can solve in our personal lives by learning about language and using it with care and imagination. The flow of our words could be as clear and fresh as the cascade of an unpolluted, free-flowing stream. We could then choose our words the way we plant a garden—thoughtfully and with an eye to beauty."[10] This is Cardinal Dolan's "language of yes."

As Fr. Martin Pable, OFM, noted, "I do not want us to deny, water down, or cheapen any of the truths we have received from Scripture, tradition, or the Church's magisterium. But I believe our message will be more effective if we try to communicate it by using the language of relationship; the language of values; and the language of meaning and purpose."[11] Our words should never minimize the real suffering and pain of human life or present a simplistic view of discipleship. We should never shy away from a difficult message, for in truth, we are never very far from the cross. But our words should remind us that even while they mourned, Jesus called Lazarus to come out of the tomb and cast aside the burial garments. The language of preaching is the language of exiting tombs. It is the language of relationship, redemption, purpose, and hope. It is also the language of the table: welcoming, abundant, and nourishing. It is language that challenges and demands but does not break the listener.

The language of "yes" is an oral language. It is language that cuts to the heart and conveys deep theological truths in a clear, evocative, and memorable way. The language of "yes" is spare, economical, and courteous. Jesus always quit talking while the people were still listening. He left room in his stories and around his images for the listener to linger and explore. He avoided pat conclusions and invited the listener to actively participate in the creation and continuation of meaning.[12]

Language formation is vital in preparing permanent deacons for effective preaching and evangelization. Deacons are woven deeply into the fabric of the community and view their fellow parishioners through the shared lens of work, family, home, and church. Ideally, they have also moved widely in the larger community and have engaged in apostolic service in the areas of justice, charity, mercy, and pastoral care. This rich tapestry provides a significant foundation for preaching. There are significant challenges as well. In my own diocese, most men enter the diaconate from a lifetime in business, the trades, technology, engineering, law, accounting, and farming. Over 75 percent of our recent candidates show personality types with strong inclinations toward introversion, thinking, and judging. The test facilitator was amazed at the number of candidates whose profile summaries included these words: serious, orderly, dislikes ambiguity, black/white thinker, logical, practical, fact-driven, organized approach, prefer to have things settled, decisive, assertive, and objective. With few exceptions, they have been well-trained in linear and analytical thought. Most have minimal experience with literature, theater, the arts, poetry, and the world of the creative imagination.[13]

To help them preach words of abundance, liberation, healing, and hope, we must first explore how these words look, sound, feel, and taste in their own cultures and communities. We must examine how the language of evangelization and preaching—the language of "yes"—differs from the language of engineering reports, financial statements, and market analysis. To accomplish this, we need to balance time spent in the study of philosophy, theology, Scripture, ethics, and homiletic methodology with equally important time spent exploring words, images, poetry, and literature. We should create the time and space needed for them to fall in love with words: to wrestle with unwieldy and disobedient words and come face-to-face with exuberant and unexpected words. Like a child clutching a helium-filled balloon, they need the experience of holding on to words that want to take flight and travel someplace new. We should help them discover words capable of evoking the mystery of life even in the midst of death. Time is a rare and precious commodity in our deacon formation programs and it can be tricky to argue that time should be reserved for poetry readings and Bananagrams. Yet, if we don't attend to language and creativity, we may just miss out on the type of preaching Pope Francis describes as "a source of living water," a "language [that] is a kind of music which inspires encouragement, strength and enthusiasm" (*Evangelii Gaudium* 139).

What follows are some practical suggestions to foster imagination, creativity, and language for preaching. These suggestions include classroom exercises as well as homily preparation approaches and material for personal reflection. In most cases, they require a sense of play, a suspension of schedules, and a willingness to wander down new paths without the security of a GPS.

1. *Begin with an understanding of silence.* It may seem counterintuitive to begin an exploration of language with an exploration of "not language," but effective speech begins with effective listening and an appreciation for the power and beauty of stillness. Pope Benedict XVI's message on World Communications Day 2012 stated, "Silence is an integral element of communication; in its absence, words rich in content cannot exist."[14] The 1997 Lyman Beecher Lectures in preaching, delivered at Yale Divinity School by Rev. Barbara Brown Taylor, opened with the question, "How shall I break the silence? What word is more eloquent than the silence itself?" Later, Taylor notes, "Our authority to speak is rooted in our ability to remain silent."[15] Pope Benedict reminded us, "The great patristic tradition teaches us that the mysteries of Christ all involve silence. Only in silence can the word of God find a home in us."[16] Our preached words should be the rich fruit of active and expectant listening. Preachers should frequently engage in the practices of meditation, contemplative prayer, *lectio divina*, and the art of attentive listening. Preachers should be encouraged to examine and uphold the vital role of sacred silence in the liturgy so that "we expect the liturgy to give us a positive stillness that will restore us."[17]

2. *Impose restrictions, limits, and boundaries to nurture the effective use of language.* Most preachers offer their listeners too many, rather than too few, words and generate multiple themes rather than one clear message. As a result, much of today's preaching feels bloated and unfocused. Brevity may be wit, but editing for brevity is an acquired skill that takes time and experience. Blaise Pascal is credited with the statement, "I have made this [my letter] longer than usual because I have not had time to make it shorter."[18] Barbara Brown Taylor speaks of "homiletic restraint" and the importance of economy, courtesy, and reverence in speech so that we choose "to say only what we know to be true, to say it from the heart, and to sit down."[19] Working within limits boosts creativity and trains preachers to select words carefully, so that each word earns its own keep. Dr. Seuss wrote *Green Eggs and Ham* after being challenged by his editor to produce a book using no more than fifty different words. Using this challenge, what can we say about baptism in fifty words? in twenty-five? in five? How can a particular homily be pruned for clarity? Which handful of words is vital? Which are expendable? Exercises that teach editing skills also teach preachers to value the power of each individual word.

3. *Explore the character of oral language.* How does oral speech differ from academic, theological, and philosophical writing in structure, sound, rhythm, tempo, and usage? Oral language is meant for the ear, not the eye. It is immediate, direct, active, descriptive, and concrete. It carries a minimum of subordinate clauses. It has a shorter rhythm and may include choppy and incomplete sentences. Oral language is lean and takes a "less is more" approach. Oral language repeats and often carries a rhythm or incorporates a pattern. It favors sensual words that help the listener see, feel, smell, hear, and taste. Oral language is not "church speak" but is both accessible and earthy. Lofty theological terms must be translated into words that are meaningful to the community. Exercises that help preachers understand the nature of oral language and attend to the biblical and liturgical texts are vital.[20]

a. Listen to song lyrics and music, particularly music meaningful or popular with your community. Bluegrass, folk, blues, country, pop, rock, and hip-hop have different oral language usage and patterns. Explore the ways artists use rhythm, alliteration, repetition, and imagery to evoke a scene or tell a story. How does this language differ from the language of written texts?

b. Read poetry, prose, and homilies aloud, choosing from a variety of styles and authors. My own list includes authors such as Maya Angelou, Wendell Berry, Dr. Seuss, Anne Lamott, Barbara Brown Taylor, Martin Luther King, and Fred Craddock. Your list should include those poets, authors, and preachers whose words inspire and challenge your ways of hearing and thinking and those who speak in the voices of your culture and community.

c. Incorporate language exercises into preaching formation. Word games such as Complete the Sentence, Build a Story (someone starts a sentence or a story and everyone adds to it in sequence), Magnetic Poetry, and yes, Bananagrams, foster language awareness and creative word usage. Place a biblical or liturgical text into a "word cloud." These computer-generated clouds give greater prominence to words that appear more frequently in the source text. Seeing the text as a visual pattern may foster unexpected connections and new insights into the language and meaning of the passage.[21]

4. *Help preachers develop the power of observation and description.* Journal exercises that use an overheard conversation, a character from Scripture, or the movements and actions of a liturgical event as a trigger can sharpen these skills. Journaling may feed the imagination and foster new ways of seeing and speaking about familiar stories, texts, and actions.

5. *Explore symbol, image, and sacramental elements.* Assign a long-term study of a liturgical action, image, or sacramental element such as water, oil, or fire. Ask, "What does history, Scripture, tradition, literature, science, poetry, cinema, art, and culture have to say about this? What stories do we tell about this?" Periodically, invite preachers to share their work. As they articulate their experience and insights they are also learning to "translate" theological truths into oral language.

6. *Facilitate sensate explorations of Scripture.* Read a passage aloud and invite preachers to reflect on what they hear, see, feel, taste, or smell. In subsequent readings, identify and chart the action verbs, the adverbs, the adjectives. What is the movement and action of the passage? How does language help it come alive? What insights emerge? How would you convey your insights to others?

7. *Use art, music, and poetry as exegetical commentary or as a prompt for theological reflection.* How does this artwork illuminate or speak to the Scripture passage? How does this experience differ from using a traditional biblical commentary? Visualize words and think in pictures. What do "redemption," "sacrifice," or "unconditional love" look like? What stories and images come to mind? How might this affect the words of preaching?

8. *Read or view something surreal or absurd*: a work of art, a movie clip, or a literary passage. Experiencing the surreal jolts us from complacency, expands our horizons, and opens us up to new possibilities. As our minds

strive to make sense of what we see and experience we may find new forms of expression.

9. *Practice "lateral thinking."* People trained in linear and logical thought tend to speak in terms of classification, analysis, and conclusion. Yet, the mystery about which we preach is not linear, nor can it be easily classified. Pushing boundaries by bringing together words, objects, and experiences that seem to be unrelated and considering how they might interact or embarking on a trip where the destination is initially unclear can foster creativity, innovation, and new ways of communication. The television show *MacGyver* featured a secret agent who escaped from ostensibly impossible situations because he was a master of lateral thinking. MacGyver was able to see egg whites not just as breakfast but as a patch for a leaky car radiator. Two candlestick holders, a floor mat, and an electrical power cord became a makeshift defibrillator.[22] An internet search of "lateral thinking" will surface suggestions and exercises.

10. *Explore the process of Appreciative Inquiry*, developed at Case Western Reserve University in the 1980s by D. L. Cooperrider and S. Srivastva.[23] Appreciative Inquiry is a change management approach that posits communities and organizations will grow in the direction of focused attention since energy follows inquiry. If we focus on problems, we become experts in finding, naming, and fixing problems. If we focus on strengths and possibilities, we become experts in recognizing, naming, and living into those possibilities. Appreciative Inquiry challenges us to use different words and ask different questions, to discover what is good and amplify the best. "We could move beyond a focus on symptoms to a deeper dialogue about the life-giving forces of the Church. Such dialogue would mirror the earliest beginnings of the Christian Church when disheartened disciples, hiding out in fear and grief, told transformative stories to one another."[24] Appreciative Inquiry reminds us to choose our words and our questions wisely, for they have the power to shape our experience of the present and our vision of the future.

According to its ordinary meaning, the word "evangelization" expresses the idea of announcing a message of joy—a reward given to the messenger of good news, or the messenger who brings these good tidings. For the Christian people, our message of joy was ultimately embodied in the life, ministry, and words of Jesus. His words continue to invite and sustain us as we exit tombs and discover life in the midst of death. What a blessing for the people of God to hear this life-giving message from messengers who embrace the language of "Yes!"

Endnotes

1. "Dolan: 'missio ad gentes' and New Evangelization," *News.va*, February 17, 2012, http://www.news.va/en/news/the-announcement-of-the-gospel-today-between-missi.

2. *Science* 317, no. 5834 (July 6, 2007): 82.

3. Karl Rahner, "Priest and Poet," *Theological Investigations*, vol. 3, trans. Karl-H. and Boniface Kruger (Baltimore: Helicon, 1967), 313.

4. This "negativity bias" is noted in numerous psychological and sociological studies. See, for example, Roy Baumeister, and others, "Bad Is Stronger than Good," *Review of General Psychology* 5, no. 4 (2001): 323–70.

5. Thomas Moore, "The Power of Language," *Resurgence and Ecologist* 264 (January/February 2011), http://www.resurgence.org/magazine/article3284-the-power-of-language.html.

6. Excerpt from Bill Moyers' Conversation with Archbishop Tutu, April 27, 1999, http://www.pbs.org/moyers/journal/12282007/transcript2.html.

7. Andrea Porcheddu, "Orwell and the Power of Language," http://www.academia.edu/721095/Orwell_and_the_Power_of_Language.

8. Mary Catherine Hilkert, *Naming Grace: Preaching and the Sacramental Imagination* (New York: Continuum, 1997), 33.

9. Bishops' Committee on Priestly Life and Ministry, *Fulfilled in Your Hearing*, 7.

10. Moore, "The Power of Language," op. cit.

11. Martin Pable, "A New Language for the New Evangelization?," *The Priest* (January 2013).

12. Barbara Brown Taylor, *When God Is Silent* (Cambridge, MA: Cowley Publications, 1998), 113–14.

13. Susan McGurgan, "Servants of Christ and Stewards of God's Mysteries: Permanent Deacons and Formation for Mystagogical Preaching" (paper presented at the Academy of Homiletics, 2012), 4–6.

14. Benedict XVI, Message for the 46th World Communications Day, May 20, 2012, http://w2.vatican.va/content/benedict-xvi/en/messages/communications/documents/hf_ben-xvi_mes_20120124_46th-world-communications-day.html.

15. Taylor, *When God Is Silent*, 3, 99.

16. Benedict XVI, General Audience, March 7, 2012, http://w2.vatican.va/content/benedict-xvi/en/audiences/2012/documents/hf_ben-xvi_aud_20120307.html.

17. Cardinal Joseph Ratzinger, *The Spirit of the Liturgy* (San Francisco: Ignatius, 2000), 209.

18. Blaise Pascal, *Lettres Provinciales* (1657).

19. Taylor, *When God Is Silent*, 99, 101.

20. Anna Carter Florence shares a variety of exercises to help preachers attend to the text. Many of these also help preachers develop their sense of language and imagination. See *Preaching as Testimony* (Louisville: Westminster John Knox, 2007), 139ff.

21. See more suggestions at www.creativitygames.net. Word cloud generators are available at www.wordle.net and www.tagxedo.com.

22. *MacGyver*: season 2, episode 19; season 1, episode 15.

23. There are many books, articles, and web resources that explore the principles and processes of Appreciative Inquiry, including D. L. Cooperrider, D. Whitney, and

J. M. Stavros, *Essentials of Appreciative Inquiry* (Brunswick, OH: Crown Custom Publishing, 2008); Diana Whitney, Amanda Trosten-Bloom, and David Cooperrider, *The Power of Appreciative Inquiry: A Practical Guide to Positive Change* (San Francisco: Berrett-Koehler Publishers, 2010). See also *The Appreciative Preacher*, a web resource that connects AI with preaching: http://www.appreciative-preacher.com.

24. Susan Star Paddock, *Appreciative Inquiry in the Catholic Church* (Plano, TX: Thin Book Publishing, 2003), 4.

Chapter 12

Black Preaching and the Diaconate: Gifts and Challenges for the New Evangelization

Melvin R. Tardy

Introduction

I'm encouraged that the 2013 episcopal document *Preaching the Mystery of Faith* highlights African American preaching. Responding to societal changes and St. John Paul II's call for a New Evangelization, it encourages more catechesis, scriptural foundation, and inculturation in preaching. To that end, the bishops note that black preaching is "rich in content and expression, relies heavily on the biblical text, and draws generously from story, song, poetry, humor, anecdote, and descriptive language."[1]

My interest in black preaching stems from my ordination to the permanent diaconate in May 2011 and subsequent assignment to my home parish of St. Augustine—a historically African American parish in South Bend, Indiana. Black homilists were then nonexistent at my parish. Still, as an African American, I was aware of black preaching's standard of excellence and that Catholic homilies rarely met that standard. Also, in content and style, the latter rarely seemed culturally relevant to blacks and other people of color.

Early on, I feared giving homilies like the latter, because few seemed to have high expectations for diaconal preaching and because my homiletic training included no African American preaching. Meanwhile, having lost a generation of black youth, our parish was shifting from predominantly black to white—and the community's cultural sensibilities were shifting along with it. I began to sense a "tension" between the voice I sought to develop and the new mainstream cultural expectations. Nevertheless, mindful of our parish's unique mission, I immersed myself into the art of black preaching. I honed my craft while adapting to this cultural dynamic—this tension—and, in fact, I've learned to embrace such tension.

Black and Catholic: A Life on the Margins

In reality, I've experienced tension between my African American race and my Catholic religion all of my life. In predominantly Catholic settings, my attempts to use African American cultural expressions bring accusations that I am not "truly Catholic"—most often, I am stereotyped as Baptist or Protestant. Around black folks, I am rebuked for not being "black enough." They argue, "How can you be Catholic? Isn't that a white, racist church?"

While growing up, this tension confused me. I thought I alone experienced it. Then, I encountered *The Souls of Black Folk*, written by W. E. B. Du Bois in 1903. Du Bois says, "It is a peculiar sensation, this double consciousness, this sense of always looking at one's self through the eyes of others, of measuring one's soul by the tape of a world that looks on in amused contempt and pity. One ever feels his twoness, an American, a Negro; two souls, two thoughts, two unreconciled strivings; two warring ideals in one dark body, whose dogged strength alone keeps it from being torn asunder."[2]

Du Bois provided me with words to interpret my existential reality—that to be black and Catholic is to experience a similar double-consciousness, an irreconcilable twoness. From the writings of black Catholic theologians like Sr. Jamie Phelps and Rev. Cyprian Davis, I learned that many black Catholics experience this same tension. It should not surprise me to encounter such tension at St. Augustine Parish. I've come to rely on what Du Bois identified as the "dogged strength" of Negroes—what black Catholics might call grace or enduring faith. After all, tension over time has produced beautiful diamonds from coal! God has a purpose for everything.

Permanent Deacon: Preaching the Experience of Tension

St. Paul says in Romans 8:28 that "all things work for good for those who love God, who are called according to his purpose." Through ordination,

I responded in a unique way to God's love. Ironically, only then did I realize that God had used the tension of my experience as a black and Catholic for good: to prepare me for the tension I now face as a permanent deacon. After all, which is the greater tension: to be black and Catholic . . . or to be married and clergy? What of my conflict between family and parish obligations, between living to serve and working for a living? As a black Catholic, I live on the margins of two worlds. I now apply Du Bois's words to a similar double-consciousness as a deacon.

But deacons not only experience the tension of twoness; we preach about it! For at Sunday Mass, when we proclaim the mystery of faith, do we not preach of Jesus as at once human and divine? Moreover, does not Mass mysteriously occur at once in heaven and on earth? At baptisms, do we not preach of dying while being born again? Do we not preach of the tension St. Paul describes of "living in the world but not of the world"? Are funeral homilies not of the tension between death and life or, as Paul Scott Wilson has observed, "between Good Friday and Easter"?[3] Do we not preach of joy in the midst of sorrow?

Finally, observe the acts of the first deacons: how they served the poor and neglected (those widows of Greek-speaking Jews); how the Holy Spirit led Deacon Philip to preach salvation to Ethiopia and Samaria— those on the margins of Jewish life; how Deacon Stephen embraced the tension of martyrdom by preaching truth to power on behalf of the oppressed. They not only experienced tension, but they embraced it. Modern deacons now minister in parishes and prisons, hospitals and homes. We prepare people for RCIA and sacraments. Deacons bring compassion and communion to the sick and dying. Like our forebears, we don't wait passively on the needy. We wait only on the Spirit to lead us to them. As we wait, we experience tension. To preach from experience, therefore, the deacon must preach of tension.

An Introduction to Negative and Positive Tension

St. Augustine Parish exists in an economically depressed African American neighborhood. Some come for the Bread of Life, others for the bread of our soup kitchen. We have lifelong parishioners and new members, especially whites, who wrongly expected our so-called black parish to be the last stop on their exit tour out of the Catholic Church. Many we encounter are experiencing something akin to a conflict zone, a place of negative tension. The conflict could be from hunger or unemployment, racism or relationships, addictions or abuse, unexpected health or financial crises, even the lonely melancholy that accompanies advanced age. Indeed, some suffer the conflict of spiritual warfare with pronounced intensity *precisely because* they exist on the margins of life.

Our role as deacons is not to recoil from such conflict, but rather, to insert ourselves into that conflict zone, in order to help them encounter the good news of Christ in the midst of their struggle. In short, our role is to introduce positive tension into the crisis, something that I see as a hallmark of traditional black preaching.

To clarify, I propose that two types of tension exist in the world: negative tension and positive tension.[4] Negative tension results from the presence of sin and evil in the world. It produces a conflict God never intended. In that conflict zone is the potential to be consumed by such conflict, to become its victim. In fact, our protective instinct is to shield others, especially those we love, from our conflict zone by hiding its existence from them. For example, people could experience hidden conflicts with pornography or drugs that, if left unchecked, have the potential to consume their health, job, relationships, and even their or someone else's future.

Conversely, positive tension results when we recognize the presence of God in our midst. It reflects our efforts to embrace the Gospel and likewise resist the evil of this fallen world. This particular tension, we must embrace. It is a sign of God's love working to transcend the barriers protecting our conflict zones, to deliver us from evil and to "work all things for good." If negative tension brings a conflict zone, positive tension brings an encounter zone—an encounter with Christ who offers grace to do God's will.

It is impossible to preach the Gospel without tension, because tension always exists between the ways of this fallen world and the message of the Gospel! Deacon Stephen preached the Gospel anyway, willing to embrace the ensuing tension with joy! We too must recognize the Good News of positive tension—in our faith lives, ministry, and preaching—and to embrace it with joy.

It is not human nature to embrace tension. Therefore, some—including clergy—have an aversion to tension of any kind. Some wrongly commend themselves for establishing a veneer of peace over true peace. Recall, however, the familiar words of Dr. Martin Luther King: "True peace is not merely the absence of tension; it is the presence of justice."[5] For at the heart of justice is the will of God. The will of God comes forth marching, cloaked in the blood of positive tension. This is why Jesus brings "not peace, but a sword." This is why, when deacons embrace positive tension, they indeed embrace a cross.

As well, deacons must not shun those suffering from negative tension. The latter crave good preaching, yearning to experience the light of the Gospel shining brightly through the protective glass of their conflict zones; yearning to replace the night of negative tension with the dawn of positive tension, the sign of God's presence and of spiritual warfare being waged and won on their behalf. Indeed, deacons who embrace victims of negative tension follow the Way of Matthew 25:40: "whatever you did for one of these least [people] of mine, you did for me."

Black Preaching: From "Keeping It Real" to "God Is With Us"

Because it is informed by African American spirituality, black preaching tends to "keep it real" by acknowledging the existence of communal suffering and the human condition. Yet, the hallmark of black preaching is its ability to see within negative tension the potential for positive tension, to encounter joy in the midst of sorrow, and indeed to celebrate in faith despite the dark clouds of conflict. As Frank Thomas explains, "Celebration is . . . where a moment is created in which the remembrance of a redemptive past and/or the conviction of a liberated future transforms the events immediately experienced."[6]

In the dark days of slavery, of Jim Crow, and of brutal racism and oppression, the descendants of Africa encountered Christ the Suffering Servant in the midst of their own suffering and they survived. An illiterate people by law, force-fed the Gospel on a dish of lies, they nevertheless learned to embrace the truth of the Gospel with joy—in secret hush arbors, ring shouts, and revivals.[7] They preached of God's love for the poor, God's power to liberate the oppressed, and the "assurance of grace"[8] to those who endure in faith. Though negative tension abounded, they hung their harps of hopelessness on a tree to instead preach the prophetic voice of freedom and justice from the mountaintop. They engaged in God's work to "transform the jangling discords of our nation into a beautiful symphony of brotherhood."[9]

The world of today craves this work, this transformation to positive tension. Young people see a world seething with conflict—conflict at home, conflict at school, and conflict on the mean streets in between. They hear it on the radio. They read it on the internet. They see it on TV. It is the lead story on the news every day. No one can escape it. As a consequence, the younger generation grows more afraid of the world even as the older generation grows more afraid of them! Negative tension is the way of the world. If humanity is to survive, we need another way. In fact, we need the Way.

Fortunately, when Vatican II revived the permanent diaconate, it also revived the legacy of powerful preaching forged by the earliest deacons. Deacons, however, should not preach too powerfully about the presence of negative tension. It is not enough to merely point out what's wrong with the world or humanity; that's hardly "Good News." Rather, as demonstrated above, good preaching focuses on positive tension, God's presence in the midst of our storms, powerfully working with us toward our salvation. Good preaching invites us to open our hearts to the manifestation of God's kingdom on earth, and to celebrate its arrival with joy.

Embracing Tension: Black Preaching and the Diaconate

Recall my joy at the mention of black preaching in *Preaching the Mystery of Faith*. Other deacons could complete my joy by sharing in some of the gifts of the black preaching tradition.

The first gift is this: a reminder that preaching itself *is* a gift. Good black preaching—with its high standard for relevant, scriptural, uplifting preaching—re-presents preaching to the world as God intended: as a gift! Here, I refer not to style, but rather, to black preaching's reputation for excellence. Deacons and other preachers prepare to the standard expected of us. The reputation established by the black preaching tradition raises the bar for all preaching. Awareness of that standard motivated me to develop as a preacher beyond the expectations of others.

The second gift is indeed the black preaching style itself, which has merit for the New Evangelization. In *Preaching the Mystery of Faith*, the bishops call for more catechesis, scriptural foundation, and inculturation in preaching, and then say that good black preaching is "rich in content and expression, relies heavily on the biblical text, and draws generously from story, song, poetry, humor, anecdote, and descriptive language" (37). The latter elements allow for flexible adaptation to diverse cultures. Black preaching's prolific use of mnemonic devices—hearkening to its African oral heritage—could lend itself well to the greater incorporation of Scripture and catechesis advocated by the bishops. Good black preaching is also interactive, deftly using alliteration, call and response, dialogical language, and repetition of thematic refrains to engage (not merely entertain) diverse listeners. As Frank Thomas explains, "In the classical rationalistic deductive method, it was as if the minister had come down from Mt. Sinai with a message from God, while the people waited passively for the revelation. But when dialogical language is used effectively, the people and the minister go up the mountain of God *together* and encounter the word of God."[10]

A third gift, advocated by Frank Thomas and Henry Mitchell, is celebratory experience. For example, Pope Francis implores the faithful to share the joy of the Gospel (*Evangelii Gaudium* 3). Joy is not easily conveyed through intellectual exercise; it is an emotion that one experiences. Who can share what has not been experienced? Thomas discourages preaching that appeals solely to rational intellect or raw emotion; its impact on core belief is rare and fleeting. Core belief resides deep within the intuitive, containing "powerful principles and assumptions" (i.e., fears, anxieties) that can resist changes in opinion or behavior. Good black preaching instead appeals primarily to the intuitive, to access and over-record the tapes of core belief, thereby opening up the possibility of "fresh encounters."[11] Ultimately, this creates a moment where one is suddenly free to experience in the present what one once possessed only in faith. The natural response to this transformative experience is joy and celebration.

Beyond style, however, Cleophus LaRue argues that the power and uniqueness of black preaching derive from a fourth gift: the black hermeneutic.[12] Blacks communally perceive God and interpret Scripture in a particular way, because of shared history and experience. We interpret God to be a powerful ally with a prophetic message of liberation for the poor and oppressed. This hermeneutic assures us of God's grace in the midst of communal suffering—that God can, as black folks say, "make a way out of no way." Through such a lens, I have preached of Deacon Philip being led by the Spirit to baptize the treasurer of the Ethiopian queen: a black man of great power and status (Acts 8:27-40). While "Ethiopian eunuch" is certainly valid, my interpretation might resonate more powerfully with communities whose depictions of black males tend to be emasculated or nonexistent.

The final gift, which I call "informed improvisation," is inspired by the synergy between preaching and jazz.[13] Like jazz improvisation, good black preaching is not simply about spontaneously creating things out of thin air as the Spirit moves you. It's an "informed improvisation," very intellectual, very emotional, involving complex preparation. The outward appearance of creative spontaneity comes from the fluency of the artist in the language and technique of jazz or (in this case) preaching due to intense "woodshedding" sessions over time: that is, honing one's unique voice by listening to the masters, transcribing their "solos," and studying their influences. It involves picking out themes and subthemes, memorizing standards, chord changes, and common riffs, and learning the right combination of notes—of tension and resolution—to move your audience.

The main challenge to utilizing the gifts of black preaching could be the one we started with: negative tension, the perception that it is not "Catholic enough" for the pulpit or homiletic and formation programs. Yet, I experience the positive tension of preaching every other week to a mixed parish of blacks and whites; a parish that defies the traditional common sensibilities of US race relations; a parish that defies the observation of Dr. Martin Luther King Jr. that the hour of Sunday worship is the most segregated hour of the week; a parish that acknowledges a history of racial missteps but marches on still to embrace the dream of a King; and a parish that is learning to embrace the tensions—and gifts—of an authentically black and truly Catholic deacon who is still developing his voice as a preacher of the Gospel. In the meantime, I'm greatly encouraged by the growing warmth of their embrace.

Conclusion

Our volume theme is "To All the World: Preaching and the New Evangelization." Indeed, the earliest Christians had a similar charge. After some success, these Hebraic Jews suddenly caught wind of some negative tension within their community of Greek-speaking Jewish converts. Although these converts had embraced the Gospel, the former repeatedly neglected the poor widows of the latter in the daily distribution of gifts, perhaps the result of a language or culture barrier, old prejudice and anxieties bubbling to the surface to cloud the Gospel message of love and inclusion. Finally, moved by the Spirit, the apostles laid hands on seven men from the Greek-speaking community itself to tend to their own. The service of these seven deacons freed up the apostles and allowed tremendous growth in the church, but it didn't stop there. When the persecution of Saul began, the Spirit led Deacon Philip to share his gifts and experiences beyond his own community—to evangelize Gentiles in Ethiopia and Samaria through his preaching and miraculous signs—and the apostles were amazed by his success! Perhaps Gentiles could relate to this deacon, a man who could preach from experience about negative tension and life on the margins, yet also about the positive tension of new life in Christ. Perhaps, in this deacon, Christ saw a suitable envoy "to all the world."

Today's deacons are similarly called to share the Gospel through our gifts of preaching, gifts that include our particular gifts from culture and experience. Let us not hesitate to humbly share such gifts for the glory of God. Therefore, let us wait on the Spirit, so that we may more humbly wait on tables. Let us serve the powerless, so that we may more boldly preach truth to power. Moreover, let us embrace tension, so we may bring Good News into the conflict zones of life. Such conflict zones cry out for a New Evangelization, for someone to preach the Good News that can transform negative tension into positive tension and build up the kingdom of God on this earth. Finally, in our response as deacons, may the particular gifts of the black preaching tradition and the powerful preaching legacy of the earliest deacons inspire each of us in our mission to "Go and announce the Gospel of the Lord" to all the world.

Endnotes

1. US bishops, *Preaching the Mystery of Faith: The Sunday Homily* (Washington, DC: USCCB, 2013), 37.

2. See W. E. B. Du Bois, *The Souls of Black Folk* (New York: Bantam Books, 1989), 3. Sr. Dr. Jamie Phelps, OP, similarly refers to this quote in *Black and Catholic: The Challenge and Gift of Black Folk: Contributions of African American Experience and Thought to Catholic Theology* (Milwaukee: Marquette University Press, 2002), 18.

3. Paul Scott Wilson, *Preaching and Homiletical Theory* (St. Louis: Chalice Press, 2004), 94. Wilson wrote of "conceiving of law and gospel in a tensive relationship that evokes a new identity in faith" as an introduction to "trouble and grace" as homiletical tools (92–94). Wilson later draws a correlation between trouble/grace and African American preaching (105–8). Therefore, it would be worth exploring a possible similar correlation between trouble/grace and what I later propose regarding negative and positive tension.

4. When I originally prepared this text, I only noted tension generally speaking. Later reflection led to this differentiation between a tension that exists due to evil and a different tension that arises from knowing and seeking to live by the Gospel.

5. Martin Luther King Jr., *The Words of Martin Luther King, Jr.*, selected by Coretta Scott King (New York: New Market Press, 1987), 83.

6. Frank Thomas, *They Like to Never Quit Praising God: The Role of Celebration in Preaching* (Cleveland: United Church Press, 1997), 31.

7. US slavery was enforced in part by teaching enslaved peoples of Africa only those passages from the Bible that seemed to support slavery, such as Colossians 3:22:

"Slaves, obey your human masters in everything, not only when being watched, as currying favor, but in simplicity of heart, fearing the Lord." Hush arbors were secret gatherings in the woods where slaves would sing, dance, and worship God, often fusing remnants of African traditional religions and Christianity. The ring shout was one such ritual. See M. Shawn Copeland, "Foundations for Catholic Theology in an African American Context," in *Black and Catholic: The Challenge and Gift of Black Folk*, ed. Jamie T. Phelps (Milwaukee: Marquette University Press, 1998).

8. Thomas, *They Like to Never Quit Praising God*, 3.

9. King, *The Words of Martin Luther King*, 96.

10. Thomas, *They Like to Never Quit Praising God*, 8.

11. Ibid., 9, 13.

12. Cleophus LaRue, *The Heart of Black Preaching* (Louisville: Westminster John Knox, 2000), 9.

13. See Kirk Byron Jones, *The Jazz of Preaching: How to Preach with Great Freedom and Joy* (Nashville: Abingdon Press, 2004); and Eugene Lowry, *The Homiletical Beat: Why All Sermons Are Narrative* (Nashville: Abingdon Press, 2012). For the record, I am a jazz trumpeter.

Chapter 13

Preaching the Resurrection:
Central Content of the New Evangelization

Jeremy Driscoll, OSB

Introduction

The most important event of human history, indeed, the most important event that has ever happened anywhere in the created universe, is the death of Jesus Christ on the cross and his being raised from the dead by the one whom he called God and Father. This event is the central proclamation of Christian faith. Everything that is Christian derives from this: a way of life, a way of prayer, a body of doctrine. If we Christians are to understand our faith and live it, we must continually deepen our grasp of what it means to say that the Jesus who was crucified has been raised up. An unimaginable new content has been introduced into our world by the resurrection of Jesus. Everything in the created order is changed by it. What was "natural" can now be played in a new key: a sweeter, stronger music that is nothing less than supernatural. The new key of resurrection takes up every melody of the old creation—from the joyous sounds of life's greatest pleasures to the heartrending cries of suffering and death—and plays it in its supernatural tones. All that was passing and destined to be lost in the natural world is transformed into a song that will sound forever in the presence of God.

Easter is the annual celebration of this totally transformative event. By our very celebration of it, extended over many days, we come under its force, we yield to its sway, we are inserted into the new life that will never end. Sunday Eucharist is the weekly celebration of this totally transformative event. Annually, in our celebration of Easter, we are renewed in our participation in the mystery of the Lord's resurrection. Weekly, in our celebration of Sunday Eucharist we are renewed in the same. Annually we prepare for Easter with forty days of Lent. We enter Easter Day by means of the liturgies of the Paschal Triduum, but these launch us into the fifty days of Paschaltide, and all this culminates in the feast of Pentecost, an unimaginable outpouring of the Holy Spirit upon the whole world.

The liturgies of the Paschal Triduum, of the whole paschal season and of Pentecost, as well as all the subsequent Sundays of the year are themselves *events*. They are strong, complex sets of rites. In all their moving and acting and speaking and singing and taking up of symbols of the strongest kind, these liturgies become *events* in the community that celebrates them. In fact, these liturgical *events* converge with the most important *event* that has ever happened: the death and resurrection of Jesus. By means of the liturgical events the community has communion in *the* event. We die with Christ and rise with him to new and everlasting life.

As we consider the role of preaching in the New Evangelization, I want to suggest to you that we are in need of a much clearer focus on the mystery of the Lord's resurrection as the principal content of the Christian message. I will not directly face with you actual strategies for constructing homilies that "sort of emphasize the resurrection a bit more." I want to come to a more foundational level of the question, one that explores the deep structure of the entire Christian message with its center in resurrection. Then I want to indicate how the liturgy in all of its constitutive parts echoes that deep structure: the deep structure of resurrection in the Lectionary, certainly one of the greatest treasures of the reformed liturgy, and the Missal of Paul VI, and the deep structure of resurrection in the liturgy of the Eucharist as found in that same Missal.

The better we understand these interpenetrating deep structures, the more mindfully we can participate in them and celebrate them. You can consider this as part of the remote preparation that needs to be in place before attempting to construct a particular homily. Any well-prepared preacher needs to know at which point within this whole context the homily of a particular day with particular texts is to be given. The homilist helps us to hear the word of God on that day and to move naturally from that to our celebration of the Eucharist. The center of the Word and the center of the Eucharist is resurrection. Our hearts and minds expand through liturgies well celebrated and well preached. *We* become witnesses of what God has done and is doing still. *We* become evidence in the world that the Jesus who was crucified has been raised up by God, and so all things are new.

Reacting to the Synod on New Evangelization

I had the privilege of participating in the synod on the New Evangelization during three weeks of October 2012. I was invited as a theologian participant and was to be at the service of the bishops gathered in the synod, particularly in the work that was done in a language group to which I was assigned with about twenty bishops from as many countries, and with several other theologians and observers forming part of the group. For me one of the high points of the synod occurred when Archbishop Rowan Williams, at that time still the Anglican archbishop of Canterbury, addressed the entire synod in the presence of the Holy Father, Pope Benedict XVI. His was a wise and experienced voice, and his talk created a palpable energy in the synod hall, evidenced by the lively exchange that followed between him and other bishop members of the synod. It is not my intention here in any way to enter into the details of that talk, even if it is something I would highly recommend to anyone wanting to think seriously and creatively about New Evangelization. I do, however, want to cite him in the way he finished his address.

He finished with a reminder that could well serve our own purposes. When we hear the term New Evangelization, there can be a temptation to think too quickly that the task is new programs and more innovative planning. Eventually it probably is. But the archbishop reminds us that "evangelisation is always an overflow of something else—the disciple's journey to maturity in Christ, a journey not organized by the ambitious ego but the result of the prompting and drawing of the Spirit in us."[1] Not the ambitious ego, he says. New Evangelization is more than just the "next best thing" in the church. Of course, we want "once again to make the Gospel of Christ compellingly attractive to men and women of our age." But if that is to happen with any authenticity and durability, it surely cannot be something produced by the ambitious ego. Rather, it will come from our being in renewed and ardent touch with what makes the Gospel compelling to ourselves. I borrow Rowan Williams's final words and apply them to our own assembly in these days: "So I wish you joy in these discussions—not simply clarity or effectiveness in planning, but joy in the promise of the vision of Christ's face, and in the fore-shadowings of that fulfillment in the joy of communion with each other here and now."[2]

To evangelize well we must be in renewed and ardent touch with what makes the Gospel compelling to ourselves. Evangelization is always an overflow of something else. Grasping at greater depth and with deeper wonder the absolute and total novelty of the divine deed that raised Jesus from the dead and gives us a share in his new life—this makes the Gospel compelling, and preaching should overflow from it.

One of the major focuses of the New Evangelization is to bring alive again the vigor of the faith in the already baptized who may not be practicing anymore or whose practice has grown lukewarm and mediocre. Once grasped and believed in, the actual content of what Christian faith proclaims is something absolutely stunning. I think one of the main tasks of the New Evangelization for the whole church is a recovered sense of clarity about what the central core of the proclamation is. That may sound obvious, but I believe we are lacking this clarity in the general day-to-day of our life together in the church and in many of our pastoral undertakings. I kept looking for this clarity to emerge during the synod and, to be honest, I must confess my disappointment that I did not see it. That it did not emerge even there is symptomatic of the need I am drawing attention to. It is a theological question that needs to be treated competently and correctly, and it is also a question of the spirituality that would flow from the center correctly and effectively identified by theology. This is why preachers study theology and think about spirituality in relation to it. This too is part of the remote preparation that precedes the construction of a good homily.

To think about resurrection I would like to begin with a story from the synod. In his intervention on the floor of the synod hall, addressing the entire assembly of bishops, Cardinal Telesphore Toppo from India told a story. To my surprise it wasn't much picked up, but it exactly caught my concerns. I think it is revealing, both the story itself and the fact it wasn't much picked up. He told of a Hindu teenager who had been hanging around the Catholic priests for some time, in a school setting of some sort. I don't remember the details of the setting. But the boy was obviously a spiritual seeker, and he was often asking questions about Christian belief. At one point one of the priests gave the boy a copy of the gospels and told him to read them and then come back with questions and reactions. The boy came back more or less flabbergasted and accusing. He wanted to be sure he got it right, and so he demanded clarification. "Jesus is risen from the dead?" he asked. "Really risen from the dead?" "Yes," they calmly answered, not displeased at his excitement. "Why didn't you tell me!" he shouted at them, astonished that they would not have told him that straight out from the start. I think this is a big lesson for us all as we consider the New Evangelization.

The Absolute Novelty of Resurrection

It seems to me that the absolute novelty of the resurrection of Jesus from the dead should be front and center in all that concerns the New Evangelization, and should be much more explicitly the thread that is invoked throughout as the content of the faith that the New Evangelization seeks to deepen and celebrate. The Hindu boy had immediately caught the enormous significance of the Christian claim. If there is no such thing as the resurrection of Jesus—or, if there is no focused talk about it—then many interesting things perhaps remain in the Christian religion: attractive ideas about God; a sense of moral uprightness; lots of charity, though it wouldn't necessarily be clear why. Jesus has an interesting message and is a clever teacher. But to use the words of Benedict XVI in his chapter on resurrection in his book *Jesus of Nazareth*, "Only if Jesus is risen has anything really new occurred that changes the world and the situation of mankind." This is the crucial question. Did Jesus really rise from the dead? If so, then absolutely everything is different, changed. Pope Benedict goes on to state the matter this way: "Whether Jesus merely *was* or whether he also *is*—this depends on the Resurrection."[3]

Let me get ahead of myself for just a second. I want to say more about resurrection and then make some applications to preaching, but right now you can see already an application, a fresh expression, if you will. We Christians need to be people who clearly live and witness to the fact that the Jesus who *was* is also a Jesus who *is*. Jesus *is* because he is risen from the dead. Let us hope that it could never be asked of us or of our parish communities or of our religious communities, "Why didn't you tell me this!?"

But let's come back a minute to the question of resurrection in itself. During the synod, insofar as I could make a contribution in my own language group, one of the criticisms I brought forward on what was happening in the general assemblies was that the bishops did not seem to be putting the resurrection front and center. To my surprise, the striking story that Cardinal Toppo told was not much picked up on, as I already mentioned. Thus, for example, I think of the beautiful title of Pope Francis's apostolic exhortation *Evangelii Gaudium*, or The Joy of the Gospel, which was an expression already being used during the synod. But it is important to remember that the joy of the Gospel cannot be vaguely rooted, as it tended to be in our talk and in the preliminary drafting of propositions, simply in a somewhat indefinite joy of "meeting Jesus" or what I would call the "preliminary and undeveloped" joy of the shepherds at Jesus' birth. Rather, it should be rooted squarely in the joy that overwhelmed the disciples in their encounter with the risen Lord. If the New Evangelization is addressed to the already baptized who have grown lukewarm in their faith—well, they know about Jesus and that he perhaps would be interesting to meet, and they have heard what they might consider the charming stories of his birth. They probably have a general sense of how "nice" he was (I have heard it put that way) and patient with sinners. What has not been stressed enough and what could gain their attention again is that the resurrection of Jesus from the dead is an absolute novelty and the distinctive good news that Christianity offers. If Jesus is risen from the dead, the situation of humanity is entirely new. As Archbishop Williams said at an earlier point in his presentation, in Jesus "it is at last possible for us to be properly human."[4] How quietly that was said. As quiet as resurrection.

Evangelizers must be capable of forcefully putting into clear relief the absolute and unexpected novelty of this divine deed, to which believers are witnesses. Resurrection raises human nature to a new ontological level. Pope Benedict dared to use the image of calling the resurrection an evolutionary leap. "In Jesus' resurrection," he said, "a new possibility of human existence is attained that affects everyone and that opens up a future, a new kind of future for mankind."[5] Christ's resurrection affects everyone and everything. It is a new kind of event with universal consequences. Jewish faith had vague notions of a resurrection at the end of time. Virtually all other religions have some sense of an afterlife. What is new in Jesus' resurrection is not only an unimaginable future glory and future share in the divine nature on the part of human beings but, also and completely unexpectedly, the breaking through into this time, this world, into our humanity of divine life and glory in the raising of the crucified Jesus from the dead; the breaking through of a share already now in that divine glory for believers who put their faith in Jesus as Lord.

The New Evangelization—with new ardor, new methods, and new expressions—must extend the consequences of this to every dimension of human existence. This is the church's task, undertaken by her many protagonists in all the fields in which the church is engaged. The same is her task in the many pastoral options that are under way in the New Evangelization. This is the content of the faith that must continually be deepened in a faith that seeks understanding, not only in theology as classically conceived in service to the ecclesial community but also in a more effective and mature catechesis where all believers can deepen their understanding of this mystery in ways appropriate to their age. Resurrection should thread its way much more explicitly through all these topics.

In talk of the New Evangelization Matthew 28:19 is often cited: "Go, therefore, and make disciples of all nations." We are reminded that we are called to obedience to the missionary command of Jesus. Yet far less often are we reminded that this is a command given by Jesus not during the course of his earthly ministry but precisely as risen Lord. This commissioning is part of the resurrection event itself, as is the promise of the risen Lord to be with us always, "even to the close of the age." The New Evangelization is not simply obedience to a vague missionary command of Jesus. It is a solemn commissioning to witness that the one who has been crucified has been raised up and is with us always. Because of this continued presence of the risen Lord, *evangelization itself is theologically established as part of the resurrection event itself.* If we don't see this and constantly refer to it in what we do, then New Evangelization is nothing more than something done by the ambitious ego, to come back again to Archbishop Williams's warning. On the other hand, this is a marvelous realization to come to, that the evangelization itself is theologically established as part of the resurrection event. Obviously, this lends from another source—a divine source—inexhaustible energy and surprising wisdom to all that we undertake to do.

When I say *resurrection*, another way of saying this, of course, is the *mystery of the cross*, in whom the Lord of glory is hid (1 Cor 2:7). The one who is risen is the crucified Messiah. The resurrection opens the mystery of the cross and reveals the glory that is already contained in the Lord's death. But the death of Jesus was not understood by his disciples during the time the events that brought it about were unfolding. Instead, it provoked an enormous crisis in the band of disciples. We should think about the fact that we know of this crisis from those who would announce the resurrection to us, from the disciples of Jesus. This is striking. That the disciples all fled and abandoned Jesus, that Peter denied him three times, that they were hiding behind locked doors after his burial, that on the very morning of his resurrection two disciples were making their way to a village named Emmaus and were speaking of their disappointed hopes in him—all this is not information that somehow unfortunately got out and regrettably puts the disciples in a bad light. No, all this is part of the announcement of the resurrection, given to us by the very people who had denied him and fled.

The perspective of the gospels is from resurrection to cross to resurrection. That is to say, if the chronology of the story obviously moves from death to resurrection, the vantage point of its telling is resurrection; and resurrection light is diffused across all the stories that the evangelists tell, beginning from Jesus' birth and even before it and passing through every dimension of his ministry.

This means that the substantial length of the passion accounts of each of the four evangelists and the crisis that the death of Jesus provoked in his disciples must form an essential part of our understanding of the mystery of resurrection. I am talking here about the deep structures of the mystery, structures that the homilist must grasp and lead his hearers to grasp. The crisis in the disciples can be summarized in three questions, and I want to suggest that the pattern of struggle revealed in these questions is the pattern of struggle that believers in Jesus today still must undergo. The questions provoked by the death of Jesus on the cross are, first, *who is God* if he could have abandoned somebody like Jesus, who had lived his whole life in a faithful turning toward the Father, in announcing his coming reign? Second, *who is Jesus* who saw this hour approaching and did not flee from it? "No one takes [my life] from me," he said. "I have power to lay it down, and power to take it up again" (John 10:18). What was he saying in the sign he made at the Supper the night before he died? "This is my body, given up for you. This is my blood . . . for you." What enabled him to walk with such freedom and with such trust toward such a horrible death? And third, *what is to become of us*, the disciples asked, if Jesus is dead? Will we not face his same fate if we remain together? All the primary relations of the disciples' lives are put in question by the death of Jesus: their new relation with God given to them through the preaching and teaching of Jesus; their relation with Jesus, whom they believed to be the Messiah; their relation with one another as the band of his disciples.[6]

"Resurrection" is not some vivid first-century Jewish way of saying we will never forget this wonderful rabbi; let's stick together and remember him. No, resurrection takes its meaning—its divine logic is revealed—as answer to these profound questions of crisis, questions that, I repeat, must be faced by every disciple of Jesus and by everyone confronted with the proclamation of his death. Resurrection has heard the questions, Who is God? Who is Jesus? Who are we? And resurrection answers, *God* is the one who did not abandon his Son. *Jesus* is the one raised by his Father and established as Lord and Messiah. And we? Who are we? *We* are his witnesses. This deed of God is known, mysteriously, in the moment of its being announced. The community of believers neither invents the message it announces nor keeps it alive on its own strength. Rather, it witnesses to what *God* has done and to what never could have been expected. It is a divine deed, infinite in its proportions.

If resurrection is the absolute novelty of Christian faith and so the heart of the content of the New Evangelization, it remains an inextricable dimension of its mystery that it cannot be announced and encountered apart from a profound encounter with the mystery of the cross, with the mystery of the crucified One, with the questions that his crucifixion provokes. New Evangelization must show the beauty and glory of the cross as the secret, mysterious cause of joy in all who suffer. The cross is the resolution of the enigmas and contradictions of which life is full. And it is the quiet, hidden, unnoticed, firm victory over the evils of our world.

Witnessing to the Resurrection

Who is a Christian? What is a Christian? A Christian is one chosen by God to witness to the resurrection of Jesus Christ from the dead. A Christian is likewise one called to an ever deeper entry into the darkness of the questions, Who is God? Who is Jesus? What is to become of us?

But if the entry into the darkness is ever deeper, then the divine answer to the questions what resurrection itself is becomes perhaps an answer more deeply received in its consequences. Around the mysteries of Jesus' death and resurrection, the Christian is summoned to enter into the terrifying and joyful paradox that the risen Lord is met precisely in the experience of his absence to all merely carnal modes of detecting him. As St. Paul exclaimed, "if we once knew Christ according to the flesh, yet now we know him so no longer" (2 Cor 5:16).

What does this mean? Saint Paul is teaching that our encounter with the crucified and risen Lord transcends the categories of our everyday experience of enfleshed beings inserted in a particular time and place. It transcends the everyday even while being present within it. A slightly silly way of explaining it would be to say that resurrection means far more than that Jesus is just up and running again: yep, he was dead, but now he's back, just like before. No, the one who was crucified has been raised up and filled with divine glory. As he himself solemnly declares in the vision that opens the book of Revelation, "Once I was dead, but now I am alive forever and ever. I hold the keys to death and the netherworld" (1:18). Who can ever say, "*Once* I was dead?" Only the risen One . . . and those who are alive in him through faith in him.

We can understand this more deeply if we reflect further about the nature of liturgy itself and its relation to the resurrection. The homily is a part of the liturgy itself and partakes of its characteristics. The paschal mystery is something that has its roots in a particular time and place. It is an event within human history: the crucifixion of Jesus Christ under Pontius Pilate. But this event unfolds into dimensions that transcend the historical particulars. The resurrection of Jesus, his glorification at the right hand of the Father, and the sending of the Spirit are all ways in which the particular dimensions of the historical event are transcended. What God has done in Jesus in one time and place becomes available in every time and place. "[I]f we once knew Christ according to the flesh, yet now we know him so no longer" (2 Cor 5:16). This is God's own doing, and it comes about through the liturgy.

What happens through the celebration of liturgy is part of the Father's glorification of Jesus, part of his gift of resurrection to the Son, where he answers the Son's prayer that all those who will believe in him through his disciples' preaching may be one with him in the glory of the Father (John 17:20). So, far from being a mere human invention, the liturgy is something that flows forth from within the divine wellspring of the paschal mystery. This is seen above all in baptism and Eucharist. These sacraments are given to us by the Lord himself and given from within the very core of the event of his paschal mystery. Jesus gives us the Eucharist as he enters into the hour of his suffering. His command "Do this in memory of me" establishes it as a means in every generation of entering with him into that same hour. And the risen Lord, as he appears in glory before his disciples on the mountain in Galilee, commands them to make disciples of all nations and baptize them in the name of the Father, the Son, and the Holy Spirit. This command is accompanied by his promise, "And behold, I am with you always, until the end of the age" (Matt 28:20).

The Christian community has been faithful to these injunctions of the Lord in every age. It has been precisely in the celebration of baptism and Eucharist (and in all the other liturgies of the church that in fact group themselves around these) that the community discovered the Lord had hidden an enormous treasure within the simple rites that he himself handed on to us. He had hidden nothing less than his own presence and power as risen Lord. When the community celebrated these rites, he the Lord was present to all its members and acting to save them, acting to bring them into the risen and glorified life that was his Father's gift to him. After the Lord Jesus had ascended into heaven, disappearing from our sight, he sent from the Father the promised gift of the Spirit. This Spirit was everywhere active in the community, bequeathing to it the gift of the Sacred Scriptures and right understanding of them, equipping all of its members to be able to say from the depths of their being, "Jesus is Lord!" The Spirit likewise bequeaths life to the sacramental forms left to the community by the Lord. The Spirit completely fills the rites the community celebrates with the power of the Lord's hour. What Jesus began in the particular hour of his mounting the cross on Calvary, the Spirit renders present in all its force and glory in every time and space.

We see, then, that the event of the paschal mystery converges with the liturgical celebration of the sacraments. The rites that the community celebrates flow from the event itself. By entering into the rites the community enters into the very event. This is a way of speaking about liturgy that is applicable to any and all of the liturgies that the church celebrates, but this is especially clear in the celebrations of the Paschal Triduum and in the community's regular celebration of Sunday Eucharist. The convergence of the paschal mystery with the liturgical celebration of the sacraments is once again *a deep structure* of which the homilist must be aware and bring into focus and clear relief in the particular community celebrating. Our bishops' document *Preaching the Mystery of Faith* offers concrete advice on developing attention to this liturgical dimension as an important part of the homily.

Concluding with 1 Corinthians 15

A useful way of concluding these reflections would be to put ourselves again under the force of the logic of St. Paul's powerful statements in the fifteenth chapter of his First Letter to the Corinthians. This entire chapter discusses resurrection. It is there that he says, "And if Christ has not been raised, then empty [too] is our preaching; empty, too, your faith" (1 Cor 15:14). I have wanted to make the same blunt point in these reflections.

As in virtually all that he writes, St. Paul is responding to a concrete situation in what he says about resurrection in this chapter. Apparently some in the Corinthian community were teaching something to the effect of "whatever it means to preach Christ as risen, it does not mean that we too shall share in the resurrection." Some thinkers in the community were perhaps offering sophisticated, more refined, Greek-thinking views of resurrection, interpreting it perhaps as merely mythical and symbolic language. To counter such an understanding, Paul begins by "reminding you, brothers [and sisters], of the gospel I preached to you, which you indeed received and in which you also stand" (1 Cor 15:1). Then he repeats to them what is certainly one of the most primitive and basic summaries of Christian faith in all of the New Testament. The core of Christian faith is found not in philosophical speculation but in the narration of events and the naming of witnesses to those events. By Paul's time this formulation was already considered traditional. He says, "For I handed on to you as of first importance what I also received: that Christ died for our sins in accordance with the scriptures; that he was buried; that he was raised on the third day in accordance with the scriptures; that he appeared to Cephas, then to the Twelve" (1 Cor 15:3-5). The list of witnesses continues, ending with Paul himself referring to his encounter with the risen Lord on the road to Damascus.

The point of Paul recalling all this for the current problem at Corinth is to establish the fact that there should be no doubt about the content of his preaching. He preaches that Jesus "was raised on the third day in accordance with the scriptures" (15:4). Then he concludes the reminder with these words: "Therefore, whether it be I or they [the other witnesses], so we preach and so you believed" (15:11). That being established (again), he faces the problem at hand. He asks, "But if Christ is preached as raised from the dead"—and there is no doubt that this is what is preached—"how can some among you say there is no resurrection of the dead?" The argument that follows is constructed on a series of "if . . . then . . . " clauses, where Paul wants to show that the consequences of denying the resurrection are drastic indeed. The first of these is of fundamental importance. "If there is no resurrection of the dead, then neither has Christ been raised" (15:13). We might have thought he would begin the other way around: "If Christ has not been raised, then there is no resurrection for us." But, no, what some in Corinth are saying has to do with the resurrection for us, suggesting that the dead we have known and, by implication, we ourselves will not be raised up, even if Christ has been. Paul's first "if . . . then . . . " clause instead immediately draws out the consequences for us of the resurrection. "If there is no resurrection of the dead," he says, "then neither has Christ been raised." It is as if he were saying in frustration, "Well, it didn't just happen to him for his own sake, any more than he died for his own sins. It is all for us. If we don't profit from it, then it means it didn't even happen. And then what are we all here for!?"

What Paul's logic in this verse—also employed elsewhere throughout his writings—showed the Christian community through the ages, as it reflected upon and deepened his insight, is that the resurrection of Jesus from the dead is ontological in its consequences. It touches *being* as such. It opens new possibilities for *being* as such. And if it does not, then this means it simply has not happened in the first place. That is the drastic consequence, and in effect it would undo the whole Christian enterprise.

More "if . . . then . . . " clauses say so. "And if Christ has not been raised, then empty [too] is our preaching; empty, too, your faith." In other words, there is no point to being a Christian if Christ has not been raised. Drastic as well is the next consequence: "Then we are also false witnesses to God, because we testified against God that he raised Christ, whom he did not raise if in fact the dead are not raised" (15:15). Once again Paul is deep inside what I have described as the ontological consequences of the question. Paul in the course of his vigorous ministry, from deep within his own Jewish roots and rabbinical training, has been solemnly testifying, in surprisingly sharp contrast to his former persecution of believers in Christ, that God has raised Jesus from the dead. But if the dead are not raised with Jesus, then Paul would be solemnly testifying to a lie and not to God, a devastating consequence for him personally and one that would require the communities he has established to admit to having been duped by a lie.

He next insists on the connection between Christ's resurrection and our own, repeating the first of his first "if . . . then . . . " clauses: "For if the dead are not raised, neither has Christ been raised" (15:16). Then he lists even further drastic consequences, and cumulatively they would create a disastrous and hopeless scenario. If Christ has not been raised, "your faith is vain; you are still in your sins. Then those who have fallen asleep in Christ have perished" (15:17-18). Everything that Christian hope and freedom and joy are made of is shattered if Christ has not been raised. We are still in our sins, which means, in effect, that we are dead and will be forever dead. And those who have already died in the flesh are really simply dead and nothing more, and there is no hope at all for them. For Paul, Christian faith is not some set of religious thoughts primarily meant to be a benefit for the present times. Paul concludes this part of the argument with a very strong thrust: "If for this life only we have hoped in Christ, we are the most pitiable people of all" (15:19).

Paul's rhetoric up to this point in the passage has been intense and consequently quite effective. He surely had the attention by now of his Corinthian community, and he should have ours as well. Everything is at stake around this question. It is a life-and-death question. It is the meaning-of-our-existence question. Having tightened the tension of the alternatives to a breaking point—are the dead raised or are they not?—Paul pivots in the course of his argument and turns the text forcefully, proclaiming again the main point, the central content: "*But* now Christ has been raised from the dead," and then adds immediately, "the first-fruits of those who have fallen asleep" (15:20). That is, he announces Christ's resurrection and adds immediately the consequences of this for us. Christ is the first raised from the dead. This is firstfruits. The rest will follow him.

Next Paul develops in positive terms a theological argument that forms the core of what I have called the ontological consequences of resurrection: "For since death came through a human being, the resurrection of the dead came also through a human being. For just as in Adam all die, so too in Christ shall all be brought to life" (15:21-22). Christ's death and resurrection does not happen to him merely as an individual—lucky him! At least he gets to rise from the dead! No, Christ is a representative human being, a new Adam. What happens to him can happen in principle to all. To say it with Pauline language from elsewhere in his corpus: in Christ *we* can die to sin; *we* can stand justified, before God, undeservedly freed from our sins; *we* can rise from the dead to new and eternal life.

Other ideas are developed around resurrection in this gripping chapter of Paul's letter, which space does not permit us to treat here. But I trust this can be enough to summarize with firm scriptural authority my central claim. Resurrection is the distinctive good news of Christian faith. "And if Christ has not been raised, then empty [too] is our preaching; empty, too, your faith" (15:14). "But now Christ has been raised from the dead, the firstfruits of those who have fallen asleep" (15:20). Resurrection is the central content of any evangelization, new or old. The message has not changed. The event whereby we are saved has not changed. Yes, new ardor, new methods, new expressions are needed for our times. "Jesus is risen from the dead?" the Hindu boy asked his Christian friends. "Why didn't you tell me?"

Endnotes

1. Rowan Williams, Archbishop's Address to the Synod of Bishops in Rome, October 10, 2012, par. 17, http://rowanwilliams.archbishopofcanterbury.org/articles.php/2645/archbishops-address-to-the-synod-of-bishops-in-rome.

2. Ibid.

3. Benedict XVI, *Jesus of Nazareth: Holy Week: From the Entrance into Jerusalem to the Resurrection* (San Francisco: Ignatius Press, 2011), 242.

4. Williams, Archbishop's Address to the Synod of Bishops, para. 3.

5. Benedict XVI, *Jesus of Nazareth*, 244.

6. I am inspired in the formulation of this paragraph and these questions by B. Standaert, *Lo spazio Gesù* (Rome: Ancora, 2004), 247.

Chapter 14

Preaching, Teaching,
and the New Evangelization

Cardinal Donald Wuerl

In this chapter, I will first of all highlight one very significant event and mention two significant documents.

In October of 2012, the synod for the New Evangelization for the Transmission of the Christian Faith took place in Rome at the request of Pope Benedict XVI. As you know, a synod is a gathering of bishops who are representative of the church throughout the entire world. The pope convokes such a meeting, and conferences of bishops around the globe elect those bishops who will attend. Much attention has been focused recently on two future synods, one scheduled for October 2014 on the family, and the additional synod on the family in October 2015. The 2012 synod on the New Evangelization concluded, according to standard practice, with a list of propositions—in this case, fifty-eight of them—which are statements of varying length, each focused on one aspect of the three-week discussion among synod members. Given the significance of the propositions, Pope Francis wove them into the document that followed in the wake of the synod.

This brings us to the apostolic exhortation of Pope Francis, *Evangelii Gaudium* (The Joy of the Gospel). In this exhortation, Francis tells us that it is precisely at the promptings of the Holy Spirit, who helps us together to read the signs of the times, that the synod on the New Evangelization for the Transmission of the Christian Faith gathered in Rome. He also highlights that the synod reaffirmed that the New Evangelization is a summons addressed to all and it is carried out in three principal settings.

Here Pope Francis cites the work of the synod and, particularly, the concluding homily of Pope Benedict on October 28, 2012. We are reminded that the work of the New Evangelization and our witness takes place in three distinct but interrelated areas:

1. The ordinary pastoral ministry, which is "animated by the fire of the Spirit, so as to enflame the hearts of the faithful who regularly take part in community worship and gather on the Lord's day to be nourished by his word and by the bread of eternal life" (15).

2. Another area is that of the baptized whose lives do not reflect the demands of baptism, who lack a meaningful relationship with the church and no longer experience the consolation born of faith.

3. Lastly, we are reminded that we cannot forget that evangelization is first and foremost about preaching the Gospel to those who do not know Jesus Christ or who have always rejected him.

Finally, I want us to recognize the importance of the 2013 document by the United States Conference of Catholic Bishops on preaching, titled *Preaching the Mystery of Faith: The Sunday Homily*. The USCCB document draws heavily on two post-synodal apostolic exhortations: *Sacramentum Caritatis* (The Sacrament of Charity),[1] following on the synod on the Eucharist in 2005; and *Verbum Domini* (The Word of the Lord),[2] which came in the wake of the 2008 synod on the Word of God in the Life and Mission of the Church. In both exhortations we are reminded of the importance of the homily as a privileged means of passing on the word of God. Here we are also reminded of the catechetical aspect of the homily: "The catechetical and paraenetic aim of the homily should not be forgotten" (*Preaching the Mystery of Faith*, 46). This emphasis on homiletic content is the result of the recognized catechetical deficiencies of the 1970s and 1980s.

It is even proposed that "during the course of the liturgical year it is appropriate to offer the faithful prudently and on the basis of the three-year lectionary 'thematic' homilies treating the great themes of the Christian faith, on the basis of what has been authoritatively proposed by the Magisterium in the four 'pillars' of the *Catechism of the Catholic Church* and the recent *Compendium*, mainly: the profession of faith, the celebration of the Christian mystery, life in Christ, and Christian prayer" (Proposition 19, synod on the Eucharist).

In line with good preaching practices as stressed in the USCCB document, I want to address the topic of the New Evangelization in preaching today under these headings:

1. Know your audience.
2. Have something to say (that is, know what you want to say).
3. Say it with conviction and enthusiasm.

Point One: Know Your Audience

Under the heading of "know your audience" would come the recognition of the context of our faith proclamation. As we undertake the New Evangelization and the presentation of the richness of the experience of Jesus and his Gospel, we must be aware of the context in which this arduous task unfolds. The context of the New Evangelization and the very reason why we need to re-propose our Catholic faith to the world is the secularism that is now rapidly enveloping our society and our Western culture. The New Evangelization recognizes that in countries where the Gospel has already been preached there is an "eclipse of the sense of God."[3] What brings a new urgency to our mission is the acknowledgment of just how widespread and profound is the new secularism. During the 2012 synod, I referred to this phenomenon as a "tsunami of secularism."

Pope Benedict XVI, during his visit to the Archdiocese of Washington in April 2008, underlined three challenges the Gospel faces in our society. In his homily at Vespers with the bishops of the United States during a meeting at the Basilica of the National Shrine of the Immaculate Conception, he reminded us that we are challenged by secularism, the materialism around us, and the individualism that is so much a part of our culture:

> While it is true that this country is marked by a genuinely religious spirit, the subtle influence of *secularism* can nevertheless color the way people allow their faith to influence their behavior. . . . Any tendency to treat religion as a private matter must be resisted. . . . For an affluent society, a further obstacle to an encounter with the living God lies in the subtle influence of *materialism*, which can all too easily focus the attention on the hundredfold, which God promises now in this time, at the expense of the eternal life which he promises in the age to come (cf. Mk 10:30). . . . In a society which values personal freedom and autonomy, it is easy to lose sight of our dependence on others as well as the responsibilities that we bear towards them. This emphasis on *individualism* has even affected the Church.[4]

But today the context also includes Pope Francis and the so-called Francis effect. What we proclaim today and the efforts to invite people to experience Jesus and his Gospel have to be seen specifically in the light of Francis's apostolic exhortation *Evangelii Gaudium*. The title of his apostolic exhortation is as much a description of him as it is the name of this document. From the moment he stepped out onto the balcony of St. Peter's Basilica on the night of his election as 265th successor to St. Peter, Pope Francis has set a vibrant tone and has become a focal point of faith renewal not only in the life of the Catholic Church but among many, many people.

Perhaps what strikes such an appealing chord is his manner of reflecting the joy of the good news of Jesus Christ. Pope Francis is not changing any of the great received teachings in the church. Rather, he is revitalizing those teachings and highlighting how we do the Gospel, how we live the Gospel message. Recently there was a television report on just how popular Pope Francis is and that his tweets are re-tweeted more than any other person. The news report indicated over ten thousand daily re-tweets of the pope's tweet. What Francis invites us to do is focus our attention on the overwhelming blessing that is the love of God in our lives and in our world. When asked to describe himself, he humbly said he was a sinner. So we all are. But he reminded us that we have all been embraced by the love of God.

We hear so much about the "Francis effect." Recently as I waited at the luggage carousel for my bag a woman who was on the same flight asked by way of starting a conversation if I had ever met Pope Francis. She described herself as a lapsed Catholic. As our conversation went on I suggested that she might want to reidentify herself as an ex-lapsed Catholic. She explained how she felt drawn to Pope Francis and his invitation to reconsider the Gospel message and the church's place in her life. She indicated that she felt welcomed. She added that part of the welcome was the sense she got that the pope was saying to her that it was not all her fault that things were not as good as she hoped they might be. We need to meet people where they are and then walk with them to Jesus.

When I listen to the pope's talks or read his homilies, I keep hearing over and over words like "go," "invite," "welcome," "embrace," "be there for and with others." We are all brothers and sisters of the same loving Father, he emphasizes, and therefore we are called to care for one another, especially the least among us—those with the most needs. There is no reason not to take on the challenge of feeding the hungry and giving drink to the thirsty, of clothing the naked and welcoming the homeless. Our preaching must convey that same sense of welcome and imperative.

The invitation of Pope Francis to a fresh way of living the Gospel in our world—a world so desperate for forgiveness, compassion, kindness, and love—is a bright ray of hope as we move forward in the third millennium. We are blessed with the most wonderful message, the best news, to bring to our listeners. When asked, "What do we have to say?" the answer is, "The proclamation that Christ is risen."

Point Two: Know What You Want to Say

A number of years ago I was invited to speak at the Catholic Center at Harvard University. The designated theme was "The Role of Faith in a Pluralistic Society." At the conclusion of my presentation, a man who self-identified as an atheist and who taught in the law school was the first to present a question. He asked, "What do you people think you bring to our society?" The reference to "you people" was to the front row of the audience that was made up of representatives of a variety of religious traditions, all of whom were in their appropriate identifiable robes. Since he was a lawyer, I asked if he would mind if I answered his question with a question of my own. When he nodded in agreement, I asked, "What do you think the world would be like if it were not for the voices of all of those religious traditions represented in the hall? What would it be like if we did not hear voices in the midst of the community saying, you shall not kill, you shall not steal, you shall not bear false witness? What would our culture be like had we not heard religious imperatives such as love your neighbor as yourself, do unto others as you would have them do to you? How much more harsh would our land be if we did not grow up hearing, 'Blessed are they who hunger and thirst for righteousness; blessed are the merciful; blessed are the peacemakers'? What would the world be like had we never been reminded that someday we will have to answer to God for our actions?" To his credit, the man who asked the question smiled broadly and said, "It would be a mess!" The church brings what it has always brought: an invitation to faith, an encounter with Christ, and a whole way of living.

Our Message—the Good News

The Gospel offers us a whole way of seeing life and the world around us. We recognize that we cannot impose this Good News of the gratuitous love of God, but at the same time, we do need to recognize that we are called to share this news, to bring it to others, to let them know of the beauty of life in Christ. We bring a fuller vision, offering another dimension to life. In the Sermon on the Mount presented in Matthew's gospel, we hear of a new way of life and how it involves the merciful, those who hunger and thirst for righteousness, those who mourn, the peacemakers, the poor in spirit. Here we learn of the call to be salt of the earth and a light set on a lamp stand.

Later in that same gospel, we hear the extraordinary dictum that we should see in one another the very presence of Christ. Jesus' disciples are challenged to envision a world where not only the hungry are fed, the thirsty are given drink, the stranger is welcomed, and the naked are clothed, but also most amazingly sins are forgiven and eternal life is pledged.

Jesus invites us into God's family. Jesus is the "only Son of God" (John 3:18). We receive our status by adoption. "As proof that you are children, God sent the spirit of his Son into our hearts, crying out, 'Abba, Father!' So you are no longer a slave but a child, and if a child then also an heir, through God" (Gal 4:6-7).

"Why do you call us brothers and sisters?" a youngster asked me after Mass. "You're not my brother." "Ah, but I am spiritually, because we are all members of God's family," I responded. After he received a nod of affirmation from his mother and father who stood behind him, he said, "Wow, I didn't know that." Then he added, "That's cool," offering his youthful declaration of approval.

The Kerygma—the Core of the Good News

Christian life is defined by an encounter with Jesus. Our proclamation is focused on Jesus, his Gospel and his Way. When Jesus first came among us, he offered a whole new way of living. The excitement spread as God's Son, who is also one of us, announced the coming of the kingdom. The invitation to discipleship and a place in the kingdom that he held out to those who heard him, he continues to offer today. This has been true for twenty centuries.

The Gospel that Jesus Christ came to reveal is not information about God, but rather God himself in our midst. God made himself visible, audible, tangible. In return, he asks our love.

Already in just one generation after the resurrection of Jesus, St. Paul could write to the Corinthians that he was passing on to them "what I also received: that Christ died for our sins in accordance with the scriptures; that he was buried; that he was raised on the third day in accordance with the scriptures" (1 Cor 15:3-4). Paul is calling the attention of the church to the living tradition passed on from those who saw the risen Lord. He is speaking of an established, verifiable tradition within the lifetime of people who could vouch for what they had seen and what they had preached. We are dealing with a real person, and there is continuity between the person who was taken down from the cross, wrapped in the shroud, and placed in the tomb and the one who is now risen from the dead and who appeared to numerous people. Part of what we have to say is the recognition that Jesus continues to be present in his church today. In fact the church is the continuing sacrament of Christ's presence in our lives today.

Pope Francis, in his general audience on June 25, 2014, reminded us, "We are Christians because we belong to the Church. It is like a surname: if our name is 'I am Christian,' our name is 'I belong to the Church.'"[5] He highlighted that "there are those who believe that they can have a personal relationship direct and immediate with Jesus Christ removed from communion and mediation of the Church." He concluded that part of his address by the simple exhortation, "Remember: being Christian means belonging to the Church."

The Church—Home of the Good News

The deepening of our faith today brings with it a renewal in our understanding of the essential role of the church. We profess our faith in God the Father, in his only-begotten Son, and in the Holy Spirit. But the same creed calls upon us to profess our faith in the one, holy, catholic, and apostolic church. It is in and through the church that we hear and appropriate the words of everlasting life.

In response to the question "How do we come to know and encounter Jesus today?" we look to the church. The answer is found in the only living witness to the Lord Jesus, the only witness who can say I was there when Jesus died, when he rose, when we ascended into heaven, and when he sent the gift of the Holy Spirit upon it. That one remaining living witness is Christ's Body, his church. It is in living continuity with that church that you and I find our connectedness to the gospels and to Christ himself.

How does the teaching of Christ get from him to us? How can we claim truly to know Jesus? These are important questions that we must answer when we recognize that God spoke in and through Jesus Christ twenty centuries ago, yet he intended the message for each of us today. The reality through which we ensure our continuity with the Lord is called apostolic tradition. It is best described as the passing on under the inspiration of the Holy Spirit of what Jesus said and did. What makes it unique is that the very passing on in this way guarantees that the saving story of Jesus is not forgotten, misunderstood, or lost from age to age, from generation to generation, from person to person.

The mediatorship of the church is the one missing essential element of faith in the lives of so many today. The church and the Eucharist—our profession of faith that includes these two essential realities—are what set us apart from most of the rest of the Christian world. Yet you cannot fully experience the life—the new life—given to us in Christ apart from these sacred realities. An element in our proclamation of the faith is the confidence we should have in the truth of our message. It is precisely our membership in the church and our continuity with its proclamation that authenticates our message. This assurance should lead us beyond the sense of hesitancy and apology for the church's message.

As I took my aisle seat on the plane, the woman in the window seat turned and introduced herself and, seeing my Roman collar, said, "Have you been born again?" "Yes," I responded, and she immediately asked, "When?" I said, "In baptism. And I have been trying to grow into that new life ever since." "Oh," she said, "you're Catholic," which led her to another question and the beginning of a conversation that lasted the entire flight. She said as a Catholic we are big on this "church thing." She recognized that that was a major difference between us. She showed me her small prayer book that had in it a number of quotations from the New Testament reminding us that we have received new life in Christ. She then asked, "Tell me about this church thing that is so important to you."

We began with Matthew's gospel and Peter's confession about Jesus that led to Jesus' announcement, "you are Peter, and upon this rock I will build my church" (Matt 16:18). As the conversation unfolded and she raised a number of significant questions, we talked about Jesus establishing his new Body, the church, how we are all invited into the family of God, how the apostles continue today in the person of bishops to lead the church, and how the work of St. Peter is carried on today by the bishop of Rome, the pope. As we landed and were taxiing up to the gate, the man in the aisle seat directly across from me leaned over and said, "Father, I couldn't help but hear this conversation. I'm Catholic and I didn't know all of that."

The homily is truly a privileged instrument that should inspire and enrich our spiritual life and at the same time help us deepen our understanding of what is the content of the faith. This insight was also expressed during the recently concluded Year of Faith that asked us to concentrate on reflecting on the articles of our faith as articulated in the Creed. The "yes" of faith is offered in response both to our encounter with the risen Lord and to his message.

Under the heading of "know what you want to say," I am including some of the theological foundations of the New Evangelization. In our reflections on the New Evangelization and preaching, a number of theological foundation stones stand out. I would like to touch on four of them.

1. *Anthropological Foundation of the New Evangelization*: If secularization with its atheistic tendencies removes God from the equation, the very understanding of what it means to be human is altered. Thus the New Evangelization must point to the very origin of our human dignity, self-knowledge, and self-realization. The fact that each person is created in the image and likeness of God forms the basis for declaring, for example, the universality of human rights. Here, once again, we see the opportunity to speak with conviction to a doubting community about the truth and integrity of reality such as marriage, family, the natural moral order, and an objective right and wrong.

2. *Christological Foundation of the New Evangelization*: As has already been noted, New Evangelization is the re-introduction, the re-proposing, of Christ. Our proclamation of Christ, however, begins with a clear theological explanation of who Christ is, his relationship to the Father, his divinity and humanity, and the reality of his death and resurrection. At the center of our Christian faith is Christ. But the Christ we proclaim is the Christ of revelation, the Christ understood in his church, the Christ of tradition and not of personal, sociological, or aberrant theological creation. As Pope Francis just reminded us, on our own, none of us could come to know the mind, heart, love, and identity of God. Jesus came to reveal the truth—about God and about ourselves.

3. *The Ecclesiological Foundation of the New Evangelization*: The New Evangelization must provide a clear theological explanation for the necessity of the church for salvation. The church is not one among many ways to reach God, all of them equally valid. While God does wish all to be saved, it is precisely out of his universal salvific will that God sent Christ to bring us to adoption and eventual eternal glory.

4. *Soteriological Foundations of the New Evangelization*: Intrinsic to the understanding of God's presence with us today is the awareness of what we mean by his kingdom. The kingdom that Jesus proclaimed and established and that is manifest in his church will reach its final fullness only in glory. The fullness of the kingdom is yet to come but it is present in its beginnings here and now.

Point Three: Say It with Conviction

But we all know that it is important not only to know our audience and to have something to say, but we must say it with conviction and enthusiasm and we must be seen as living witnesses to the truth of what we say. We are often reminded of Pope Paul VI's maxim in his apostolic exhortation *Evangelii Nuntiandi*: people pay more attention to a witness of the faith rather than just a teacher, and if they pay attention to the teacher it is because he is also a witness (41).

Qualities of the New Evangelizers

I want to note some of the qualities required for the homilist, the preacher of the faith, in the context of the New Evangelization and what I am convinced is a moment of new Pentecost. There are many that can be identified but four stand out: boldness or courage, connectedness to the church, a sense of urgency, and joy.

In the Acts of the Apostles the word that describes the apostles after the outpouring of the Holy Spirit at Pentecost is "bold." Peter is depicted as boldly standing up and preaching the Good News of the resurrection; later Paul takes up the theme and, in frenetic movement around the world accessible to him, he boldly announces the Word.

Our enthusiasm for the faith and our conviction for its truth should always be expressed in love. As St. Paul reminds us, we must not only speak the truth but do so in love (Eph 4:15). It is not enough that we know or believe something to be true. We must express that truth in charity, with respect for others, so that the bonds between us can be strengthened in building up the church of Christ.

As our Holy Father, Pope Francis, has reminded us and as the synod pointed out on many occasions, people are not brought to the love of Jesus Christ by angry denunciations. As is being demonstrated around the world, the response to Pope Francis and his message of "loving invitation" is extraordinary. He tells us, "A Church which 'goes forth' is a Church whose doors are open." Our faith convictions "have pastoral consequences that we are called to consider with prudence and boldness" (*Evangelii Gaudium* 46, 47).

The evangelizers for the New Evangelization also need a connectedness with the church, her Gospel, and her pastoral presence. The authentication of what we proclaim and the verification of the truth of our message that these are the words of everlasting life depend on our communion with the church and our solidarity with its pastors.

Another quality of the New Evangelization and, therefore, those engaged in it, is a sense of urgency. Perhaps we need to see in Luke's account of Mary's visitation of Elizabeth a model for our own sense of urgency. The gospel recounts how Mary set off in haste in a long and difficult journey from Nazareth to a village in the hill country of Judea. There was no time to be lost because her mission was so important.

Finally, when we look around and see the vast field open, waiting for us to sow seeds of new life, we must do so with joy. In one of the final presentations of the synod, a woman from Africa, one of the auditors at the synod, reminded all of us that we need to smile when we teach the Good News. She added, "Even bishops can smile." Pope Francis begins his apostolic exhortation *Evangelii Gaudium* with the reminder that "the joy of the Gospel fills the hearts and lives of all who encounter Jesus. . . . With Christ joy is constantly born anew" (1).

Our message should be one that inspires others to joyfully follow us along the path to the kingdom of God. Joy must characterize the evangelizer. Ours is a message of great joy: Christ is risen, Christ is with us. Whatever our circumstances, our witness should radiate with the fruits of the Holy Spirit including love, peace, and joy (cf. Gal 5:22).

Conclusion: "You Will Be My Witnesses" (Acts 1:8)

Each one of us is privileged to be called and, in the context of the church, to be empowered to be a witness today to the risen Lord. At the very core, however, of our conviction is our faith. It is our Catholic faith that we proclaim with renewed adherence, awakened conviction, and great joy. It is summed up in the simple acclamation: Christ has died, Christ is risen, and Christ will come again.

Endnotes

1. Benedict XVI, *Sacramentum Caritatis* (The Sacrament of Charity) (Vatican City: Libreria Editrice Vaticana, 2007), http://w2.vatican.va/content/benedict-xvi/en/apost_exhortations/documents/hf_ben-xvi_exh_20070222_sacramentum-caritatis.html.

2. Benedict XVI, *Verbum Domini* (The Word of the Lord) (Vatican City: Libreria Editrice Vaticana, 2010), http://w2.vatican.va/content/benedict-xvi/en/apost_exhortations/documents/hf_ben-xvi_exh_20100930_verbum-domini.html.

3. John Paul II, *Evangelium Vitae* (The Gospel of Life) (Vatican City: Libreria Editrice Vaticana, 1995) 21, https://w2.vatican.va/content/john-paul-ii/en/encyclicals/documents/hf_jp-ii_enc_25031995_evangelium-vitae.html.

4. Benedict XVI, Address at the National Shrine of the Immaculate Conception, Washington, DC, April 16, 2008 (emphasis added), http://w2.vatican.va/content/benedict-xvi/en/speeches/2008/april/documents/hf_ben-xvi_spe_20080416_bishops-usa.html. (Cf. Benedict XVI, *Spe Salvi* [Vatican City: Libreria Editrice Vaticana, 2007], 13–15.)

5. Francis, General Audience, St. Peter's Square, June 25, 2014, https://w2.vatican.va/content/francesco/en/audiences/2014/documents/papa-francesco_20140625_udienza-generale.html.

Contributors

Karla Bellinger is founder and director of the Center for Preaching, Evangelization, and Prayer in Wadsworth, Ohio (www.thecenterforpep.com).

Michael Connors, CSC, is director of the John S. Marten Program in Homiletics and Liturgics in the Department of Theology at the University of Notre Dame.

Jeremy Driscoll, OSB, is professor of theology at Mount Angel Seminary in Oregon and at the Pontifical Athenaeum Sant'Anselmo in Rome.

Virgilio Elizondo (†2016) is professor of pastoral and Hispanic theology at the University of Notre Dame.

David Garcia is director of the Old Spanish Missions of the Archdiocese of San Antonio, Texas, and senior advisor for Clergy Outreach for Catholic Relief Services.

Curtis Martin is founder and president of the Fellowship of Catholic University Students in Denver, Colorado (www.focus.org). In 2011, Pope Benedict XVI appointed him as a consulter to the Pontifical Council of the New Evangelization.

Susan McGurgan is director of the Lay Pastoral Ministry Program and assistant professor of pastoral théology at the Athenaeum of Ohio in Cincinnati.

Hosffman Ospino is assistant professor of Theology and Education at Boston College, School of Theology and Ministry, where he is also the director of Graduate Programs in Hispanic Ministry.

Timothy Radcliffe, OP, author and itinerant preacher and lecturer, was the master of the Order of Preachers (Dominicans) from 1992 to 2001.

Donald Senior, CP, is professor of New Testament and president emeritus of Catholic Theological Union in Chicago, Illinois.

Jude Siciliano, OP, taught homiletics at the Graduate Theological Union in Berkeley, California. He maintains a web page (www.PreacherExchange.com) for preachers.

Melvin Tardy is academic advisor in the First Year of Studies at the University of Notre Dame, and serves St. Augustine Parish in South Bend, Indiana.

Paul Turner is a liturgical theologian and pastor of St. Anthony Parish in Kansas City, Missouri.

Honora Werner, OP, is director of the DMin in Preaching program at Aquinas Institute of Theology in Saint Louis, Missouri.

Cardinal Donald Wuerl is the archbishop of Washington, DC. He is the author of *New Evangelization: Passing on the Catholic Faith Today* (Our Sunday Visitor, 2013).